Do Your
GIVING
While You Are
LIVING

INSPIRATIONAL LESSONS ON WHAT YOU CAN DO TODAY TO MAKE A DIFFERENCE TOMORROW

Edie Fraser AND Robyn Spizman

MORGAN JAMES PUBLISHING • NEW YORK

Do Your GIVING While You Are LIVING

ISBN: 978-1-60037-452-4 (Paperback)

Library of Congress Control Number: 2008927558

Published by:

MORGAN · JAMES
THE ENTREPRENEURIAL PUBLISHER™
www.morganjamespublishing.com

Morgan James Publishing, LLC
1225 Franklin Ave Suite 325
Garden City, NY 11530-1693
Toll Free 800-485-4943
www.MorganJamesPublishing.com

Cover Design by:
George Foster

Interior Design by:
Rachel Lopez
rachel@r2cdesign.com

Author Photo by:
Keiko Guest Photography

CONTENTS

Chapter 6—Caring about Kids and Kids Who Give Back

ACKNOWLEDGMENTS

Our heartfelt thanks to the giving and talented individuals who graced this book with their hearts of gold. Thanks to each of you, this book became a reality and found a very special home.

To our outstanding publisher, David Hancock, and his talented staff at Morgan James Publishing, including Jim Howard Margo Toulouse, and Megan Washburn. We are honored to have such a dedicated publisher who is representative of the core values of giving back and making a difference. Our endless thanks to Rick Frishman who is our devoted friend and supporter at Morgan James. To our talented literary agent, John Willig, of Literary Services, Inc., we thank you for your infinite wisdom and helping to make this book a meaningful success. Your generosity and bright ideas are greatly appreciated.

Our endless gratitude also goes to Evelyn Sacks whose round-the-clock efforts and research talents supported us at every turn. Evie rose to the occasion to help us assemble a gift of literary importance, and her presence was a guiding light as we interviewed individuals, nonprofits, and corporations around the country. We also thank

Jack Heffron for his support of this mission and manuscript. To Catherine Ramsey for your editorial review and outstanding help. Casey Golden, President of the Small Act Network, we thank you for your important research in chapter 9 about technology and giving. Your work makes us realize the power of technology, and your contributions continue to inspire us as Web resources are used by millions. You advised us about important issues as well. You're the real thing and the next generation of givers!

To Tena Clark, CEO of DMI Music, music producer, and celebrity confidante, thanks for your assistance in recommending key contributors and your ongoing supporting for taking this work to the next step. You are one of the most generous individuals we know. We thank you from the bottom of our hearts for taking your valuable time to transform this book. Thank you to George Foster of George Foster Covers who helped us impeccably communicate our message. We are grateful to George for his design talents and willingness to help share our mission in such a visually inspiring way.

Our ongoing thanks goes to The Spizman Agency public relation's firm, led by Robyn's husband, Willy Spizman. You spread the message effortlessly to the media, and we thank you for your company's support sharing our book's mission and goals to make a difference in lightning speed. And to our families, Edie's dad, Les Fraser, who approaches one hundred years old and continues to give. To Edie's husband, Joe Oppenheimer, for his support and own dedication to philanthropy and volunteerism with board leadership of organizations such as Iona Senior Services and the

Bell Multicultural High School. To Robyn's parents, Phyllis and Jack Freedman, who have devoted their entire lives to giving back to the community with integrity and an abundance of dedication. To Robyn's husband, Willy, and their dedicated children, son Justin and daughter Ali Spizman, for their support of the limitless days and hours we spent on this book. And to Ali Spizman, who helped raised almost $500,000 for the Make-A-Wish Foundation to help grant wishes for medically challenged children. To Genie and Doug Freedman, Sam and Gena Spizman, Lois Blonder, Ramona Freedman, Bettye Storne, Jack Morton, Angie Perry, and a list of adored and devoted friends and family—you know who you are and play a very special role in my life. Thank you for your inspiring feedback, support, and lives of giving.

To Ben Maddox, who is with Teach for America and worked with Edie this summer, thank you for your countless hours of input and presentation. Thanks to Larry Robertson, Sam Horn, and Ofield Dukes as you introduced us to key contributors, and our appreciation to Marc Pollick for your special inspiration with the Giving Back Fund. As we thank you, we think of the passion of all of those interviewed. To you and your attentive and helpful staffs, to your devotion to giving, thanks for inspiring us. To Joyce Russell, President of Adecco; Lois Cooper, Vice President, Adecco; Rohini Anand, Senior Vice President, Sodexo; Sheela Mirmira, and so many others at AARP; to United Way and the National Urban League, John P. Moses, Chief Executive Officer of St. Jude Children's Research Hospital and ALSAC and Ken Ferber, Senior

Vice President and Chief Communications Officer of St. Jude Children's Research Hospital & ALSAC and all of the interviews included in this book, you inspire us. As we add up the hundreds of millions of members who are giving time and dollars, we are in awe of today's giving and tomorrow's thriving because of the best of human kind.

To the world of contacts and unsung heroes it took to make this book possible, we send our gratitude for helping us coordinate the leading edge thinkers in the philanthropic world. We thank these ambassadors of good will who helped us fulfill our vision. We could never have accomplished writing this book without you.

INTRODUCTION

We ourselves feel that what we are doing is just a drop in the ocean. But the ocean would be less because of that missing drop.

—MOTHER TERESA

We believe the most important word in our vocabulary, or any language for that matter, is *love*. We're not talking about love in the traditional, romantic sense of the word. Rather, we're referring to the type of love that opens our hearts to others and expects nothing in return. **It inspires us to do kind and caring things even when no one is watching.** This kind of love inspires us to spread kindness to people and places we don't know and to corners of the earth we might never see, creating a spirit of giving that has no end. This kind of love inspired us to write this book.

An act of selfless giving and loving kindness touches someone else, and the continuum of giving spreads without boundaries. We call this type of giving "inspired giving," and in this book you will find a sampling of stories of individuals, organizations, and leading-edge thinkers who are making a significant difference by giving in such meaningful and powerful ways. Through inspired giving, the human spirit allows us to rise above any circumstances and help another human being because of the bond we all share. The returns and dividends we receive change our lives. The infectious spirit of another person's gifts of time, money, or support ultimately attracts more good and deepens the bond between us.

We hope this book inspires you to do something now—to care about thy neighbor as thyself. When you give from your heart, it feels so extraordinarily good it spills all over everyone around you. *Do Your Giving While You Are Living* defines in the truest sense what a life of integrity, dignity, and value looks and feels like while celebrating the essence of giving. In understanding philanthropy and the act of purposeful giving, we discover the person we want and hope to be. When we discover the joy that comes from making a difference in other's lives, we ultimately learn that we are equally making a significant difference in our own.

Perhaps you are looking for a way to make a difference, to find a greater sense of meaning and purpose in your life. That search motivated you to pick up this book. We wrote this book with you in mind. Throughout this project we had the incredible opportunity to meet such compassionate people who are stirring souls and making a significant difference. These individuals know the true meaning of giving, and we were moved deeply by what they told us. In every corner of the earth someone is giving and doing amazing things, yet someone else is still suffering, still crying for help. As we pursued our path, we kept these questions in mind: Who will speak out for those who cannot speak out for themselves? Why should we give now? How can we better inspire others to want to give? True givers can show us the way, and in the stories you'll find in this book, they will guide you.

It's easy to block the harsh face of poverty, hunger, and homelessness, along with endless maladies, but we are certain that when you give in the most authentic sense of giving—without expecting anything in return—you, too, become an inspired giver. You become one of those individuals who help to motivate a universe of giving. Yes, our mission is clear as is our message: *Do your giving while you are living.* And when you want to make a contribution to humankind, never let anything stand in your way.

As you read this book, please keep in mind that for every person and nonprofit organization that we've included in this book, there are endless others who are making a difference by doing equally amazing feats. There are also many anonymous donors and supporters who we will never know spreading amazing acts of kindness one by one. We salute those individuals and a world of causes. The stories and people we selected to be featured in this book touch a nerve that needed probing.

We thank you for reading this book and then sharing it with someone else. In the spirit of our mission to encourage you to give until it helps, we hope you'll join us and *do your giving while you are living.*

-Robyn Freedman Spizman and Edie Fraser-

Do Your Giving While You Are Living©

If you caught him by glance but didn't see
the man who had nothing to eat.
Or turned your head and looked the other way,
to avoid the homeless on the street.

If you shield your eyes when you pass the steps
where a person in need was sleeping.
If you didn't notice the streaming tears
of a kind heart who was silently weeping.

If you never have witnessed a tragedy
and live life without deeply feeling.
Then how will you improve other people's lives
who need your support and healing?

And if you only look at heartache
with an indifferent empty stare.
Then how will you tell the next generation
why any of us should care?

You can live a life never knowing
of unfortunate stories told.
You'll never have to feel the pain
of standing barefoot in the cold.

But goodness arrives and reminds us that
we have a chance to give a new start.
To help someone begin tomorrow
with hope inside their heart.

We must hold the hand of the child in need
and lift the soul of a struggling mother.
And help someone who has been abused
and then encourage one another.

Take a stand to confront hunger
and don't allow it to persist.
And feed the world with so much love
that suffering won't exist.

We must strive hard enough to heal the sick
and ease their hurt and pain.
Provide shelter to help those escape
and come inside from the pouring rain.

Our blessings appear and remind us
to make someone's burden a little lighter.
To discover how our life gets better
when we make someone else's brighter.

As you spend your days on earth
determine the purpose for how you're living.
Will yours be a life of taking?
Or will your life be filled with giving?

Chapter 1

Why Giving Matters

Giving matters! Consider for a moment the reasons why you give. What motivates you? Do you usually make a donation because someone you know or value asks you? Do you volunteer your time or offer your help because you want to give back to the community and do your share? Do you give because some illness afflicted you or someone you love, and you now feel it's necessary to support that cause? Or, is it possible that you give because you have tapped into a deeper understanding of how to lead a more fulfilling and purposeful life?

When we give because others ask us, our giving is a tribute to those who work hard and do the asking. However, when we give because we ask it of ourselves and open our own hearts, the act of

1

giving changes our lives. In this book, we call this type of giving "inspired giving."

There are many ways to define the essence of giving. No one way is right or wrong, but inspired giving ultimately benefits both the giver and receiver and has powerful consequences for everyone involved. Inspired and purposeful giving also addresses the roots of a problem and seeks to better address its prevention rather than just its symptoms.

Understanding why giving matters in a spiritual way is one goal of this book. Examining why giving is life's greatest joy and why acts of compassion are crucial to our existence is the other. We do not want to oversimplify the act of giving. Instead, we hope to introduce you to the reasons people give on a deeper level and focus on the reasons that matter most.

As we wrote this book, what fascinated us most was the depth at which some people find themselves compelled to live a more purposeful life through giving. It amazed us that those individuals who had very little and were closest to a malady or potential problem in some cases gave more than those who had the resources or time as well as the money but not the connection.

Many of us are silently appointed in life to give back because life deals us a challenge or an unfair break. How we deal with that incident, be it an illness or a tragedy, defines us on a higher level. These are the people who show us what it means to be courageous and compassionate. We recall the young mother who lost her child to a car accident and became involved in Mothers Against Drunk

Drivers. We remember the businessman who was raised on the streets and returned to his roots to make life better for those people who are now in his same shoes. Or, how about the woman who feeds the hungry and devotes herself to that cause because she once knew a life of hunger?

Their courage and grace under fire inspires us. An illness or tragedy can shake up our spirit and motivate us to help others who suffer in a similar way. However, many individuals receive this call without a tragedy or motivating experience and respond because it's the right thing to do.

It's not just important to determine why giving matters, since we all know that it's good to give. What really counts is, how do you define your personal relationship with giving? What type of giving lights a fire in you so deep that it finds its way to brighten someone else's life? And lastly, what type of giving touches you in such a profound manner that in those simple acts of doing for someone else you discover that the light has ultimately brightened your own life in return? The star quality in this chapter makes us proud they are living a life of giving and know that all of us can emulate them with our own passion for giving.

HELP PEOPLE LIVE THEIR BEST LIVES
Caren Yanis, Executive Director,
Oprah Winfrey Foundations

OprahsAngelNetwork.org—OAmbassadors.org

"For as long as I have a voice in this world," says Oprah Winfrey, "my promise to children who have no voice is that they will be seen, they will be heard—because they matter." Creator of two foundations and a public charity, Oprah is one of the most visible and admired givers in the world.

The Oprah Winfrey Foundation is her private foundation, and The Oprah Winfrey Leadership Academy Foundation operates the Leadership Academy for Girls in South Africa. Her public charity—Oprah's Angel Network—gives her audience the opportunity to share in her enormous vision and profound ability to change lives. To help people live their best lives, Oprah's Angel Network uses donations to award grants to not-for-profit organizations around the world that are improving access to education, developing leaders, protecting basic rights and creating communities of support. Through personal and corporate donations to the Angel Network and her foundations, millions of caring people all over the world join with Oprah in this life-changing work. The beneficiaries are many. Hundreds of children enjoy the beautiful new Boys & Girls Club in Kosciusko, Mississippi (Oprah's hometown). Thousands of families throughout the Gulf Coast are benefiting from new homes and community improvement projects. Countless children around the world, from South Africa to Afghanistan to Ecuador, now have the chance to learn, thanks to schools funded through the Angel Network and the foundations. Recently, O Ambassadors launched. A joint project of Oprah's Angel Network and Free the Children, O Ambassadors is a leadership program that inspires young people to be active, compassionate, and knowledgeable global citizens.

Caren Yanis began her association with Oprah in 2000 shortly after *The Oprah Winfrey Show's* Angel Network segment evolved into a public charity. Prior to that, Caren worked with major magazines on social service projects and promotions. She is a dedicated volunteer who sits on a number of boards.

> *Every one of us gets through the tough times because somebody is there, standing in the gap to close it for us.*
>
> —OPRAH WINFREY

Watching Oprah Winfrey in action has been a life-changing experience. Oprah has an enormous giving heart and boundless empathy for people who have potential. For her, it's all about providing opportunities to help people lift themselves up. One of my favorite quotes is by Lawrence Kushner who says, "Entrances to holiness are everywhere." To me, that means going through life looking for doors that—if we go through them—could change a life or change our own lives. That's really Oprah's message—be ready to walk through that door, experience it fully, and give back however you can.

We've been working on projects in Africa for a number of years; in 2002, our ChristmasKindness initiative brought joy to kids in sixty-three schools in two provinces. They enjoyed a beautiful lunch underneath an enormous tent and went home with backpacks filled with toys, books, and supplies. This initiative moved many from Oprah's audience and beyond to make generous donations, and with these funds, we were able to return to those same schools and do things like create small libraries and provide teachers with supplies and training. We also spent time with teachers and principals at hundreds of schools in Africa to identify children who had been orphaned, mostly by the effects of HIV and AIDS. Many of those kids were young—six, seven, eight years old—being raised by siblings who were not much older, with few clothes, with little of anything, really. The Angel Network provided more than 18,000 of these young people with uniforms so they could attend school. One principal whose students received the much-needed uniforms wrote us saying: "Now my children can sing in a choir and feel proud. Now they feel they are accepted and part of a community." A new uniform and pair of shoes worked miracles that went well beyond the purpose of getting clothes on the backs of these kids so they could attend school. To see first hand the resilience and energy and hope out there gives you a perspective that goes way beyond 'poster child' philanthropy—it really supersedes the conspicuous consumerism we see every day in this country.

The foundations also give the *givers* the chance to lift themselves up. Whether it's on the Gulf Coast or in Africa, I don't think any of us have ever walked away feeling we've given more than we've gotten. When you work toward social change the return is huge, and it often comes from a place you don't expect.

Don't be afraid to step up to the plate to create social change you believe in! One of the worst things people can say is, "I'm just one person, and I can't affect change." Oprah's philosophy is, I'm doing what I can do, now you go do what you can do. Everybody can affect change by learning about the issues and then speaking out. Or maybe by getting together with friends and starting a giving circle where you all come together once a month to address shared causes and passions and learn from one another. Friends then commit to a contribution—maybe it's just $10 a month or maybe much more, but the idea is to commit. Certainly, you don't have to have a TV show to make a difference; reach out at a dinner party or to your carpool to engage others in a cause you believe in. One wonderful woman wrote us about finding $5 on the ground as she was getting out of her car in a Wal-Mart parking lot. She picked up the bill, looked up toward heaven, and said, "I know God sent this to me to send to Oprah's Angel Network because she'll know what to do with it."

Traveling with Oprah, we've been received with such love. She has such enormous compassion and respect for people in such dire situations. We've visited communities built on garbage dumps and shantytowns where the homes are all in complete disrepair. When we're invited into one of these homes, Oprah will sit down and take someone's hand, look them in the eye, and really listen to their story.

As Americans, we're often drawn to the idea of helping individuals reach their dreams, but what's often needed is a change in the system, getting to the root causes of poverty, hunger, and hopelessness. The Seven Fountains Primary School in South Africa was one of the schools we visited as part of the ChristmasKindness initiative. When we first visited the students of this school, they were learning in a well-cared-for building on a beautiful farm. But soon after we visited, their situation changed. With too many children attending the school, they were forced to relocate to a run-down building that had no electricity and no running water. Again, with the help of generous donations to our Angel Network, we were able to put together a resource team that included an architect, engineers, and educators. After a year of really getting to know the community and assessing its needs, goals, and dreams, we started to build a new school. The team even trained and then employed a group of local women to make bricks for the school by hand. An important thing to keep in mind is that the school was built for the same amount of money the government would have spent on a similar school, but it had electricity, water, a library, a computer classroom, and sports fields—all things which many impoverished South African schools do not have.

We're now partnering with the South African government to build more schools using the same approach. Built on the hope of the local community, these schools offer security and safety and provide resources that benefit the entire community. We're reminded all the time that just because you don't have resources doesn't mean you don't have ability, creativity, humanity, and spirit. This work is about connecting as human beings, not as givers and recipients.

MAKE A DIFFERENCE TODAY

Challenge yourself to learn about the underlying reasons for a social problem you care about. Read widely, find people who understand the problem and can share with you what they know. Consider starting a giving circle to commit to a cause you care about. Talk with your local school or your child's teacher about starting an O Ambassadors Club.

For more information, visit: OprahsAngelNetwork.org and OAmbassadors.org.

WHAT THE WORLD NEEDS NOW
Dionne Warwick, World-Renowned Musician and Philanthropist

Dionne Warwick is one of the world's most accomplished musical icons and devoted humanitarians. With a celebrity star on the Hollywood Walk of Fame, she is dedicated to working with organizations that empower and uplift people in need. Her work as a socially conscious and concerned global citizen has prevailed throughout her career. Beginning with the acclaimed *Don't Make Me Over* in December 1962, she has entertained audiences on every continent around the world with nearly sixty charted hits. She helped lead the music industry in the fight against AIDS, performed in 1984 at Live Aid, and was one of the key participants in the all-star charity single We Are the World. Warwick's Grammy-winning single That's What Friends Are For raised millions of dollars for AIDS research; throughout the 1980s, she proudly served as a U.S. Ambassador for Health.

In 1997, Warwick received the Luminary Award from the American Society of Young Musicians. That same year, she joined General Colin Powell in celebrating the tenth anniversary of Best Friends, an abstinence and character-building program for young women. She has served as FAO Ambassador of the United Nations, received a lifetime achievement award from the R&B Foundation, and was one of the 2003 Top Faces of Black History. In honor of her devotion to making a difference, her elementary school in East Orange, New Jersey,—Lincoln Elementary— honored her by being renamed The Dionne Warwick Institute of Economics and Entrepreneurship.

> *He who lives in harmony with himself, lives in harmony with the universe.*

> —MARCUS AURELIUS

I was brought up with the belief that giving is a part of life. Being able to be of service to those who are not capable of serving themselves is so important. I learned this from my family and my grandfather, who I always say was the wisest man who ever walked the earth. To give and to share is a blessing in itself. Those are the things that I learned as a small child and I passed on to my children. Today they are passing it onto theirs.

One of my primary concerns has always been to educate others about health issues. You have to have health to survive. I have been speaking for thirty-five years for the ones without a voice. We must all focus on the art of loving, giving, and caring. These are words that are given to you, and it's time to make them principles, for they are a must.

When I think of my music, it's hard to pick one song that defines giving, since I treat all of my songs like my children. If I had to choose one, I'd say that *What the World Needs Now* personifies God, and God is love.

I could never imagine a world without music. Music is power. We would be lost souls without it. Music is a healer, and I know this to be true. I've been told my music has been used in hospices, hospitals, and homes for the elderly. It has a soothing quality; the lyrics are so meaningful to me, and they carry a message of healing. The music industry is filled with major healers, especially from my era.

When people wonder what can they do to make a difference, I believe it's the smallest things that bring the greatest joy. A smile is one of the kindest things a person can give another—starting with the simple question, "How *are* you?" That registers with people, and I know it makes me feel good when people ask how I am doing or people smile at me. It doesn't have to be giving away a million dollars, though that might help, but it's the tiny things that matter, too.

I don't consider myself a philanthropist. I see myself as a doer. My motto has always been, "If you can think it, you can do it!" One of my greatest pleasures is that I now have the complete pleasure of watching the elementary school named in my honor. Seeing my babies being creative and energetic about learning is such a joy. Seeing the gleam in their eyes to learn and move forward knowing that there is something wonderful at the end of the tunnel—it's amazing and wonderful. Every time I go to the school to visit, I sneak in unannounced and watch from the back of the room. It's something that will live on long after I'm gone, which is a wonderful thing to think that this little girl who went to Lincoln school now has seven hundred children going to a school in her name. My hope is that that they will always remember that about me; that I, Dionne Warwick, was there for them.

MAKE A DIFFERENCE TODAY

One of the most effective ways of giving is to perfect your innate talents and pursue your passions. When you are good—really good—at something, you inspire others by your excellence. Along the way be willing to mentor, teach, and inspire those who are interested in the same things that excite you. The shared connection is a very powerful form of giving.

A Declaration of Giving
Norman Lear, Social Activist and Philanthropist

NormanLear.com

Norman Lear has sustained an amazing career in television and film, as a political and social activist, and philanthropist. He began his distinguished writing career in 1950 when he and his partner, Ed Simmons, were signed to write for the Ford Star Revue, starring Jack Haley. He produced huge hits such as *All in the Family, Good Times, The Jeffersons, Sanford and Sons,* and *Mary Hartman Mary Hartman* among many others. In 1980, he left television and formed People for the American Way, a nonprofit organization designed to speak out for Bill of Rights guarantees and to educate, energize, and equip Americans to build a country that more fully reflects the values of freedom, fairness, and opportunity in a diverse democratic society. In 1989, he and his wife, Lyn, co-founded the Environmental Media Association to mobilize the entertainment industry to become more environmentally responsible. In 1997, they formed the Lear Family Foundation, a private foundation to support a wide range of nonprofit organizations across the country.

In 2001, the Lears created the Declaration of Independence Road Trip, an educational initiative and national multimedia tour of one of the surviving original copies of the Declaration, which they own. As part of the project, Lear launched Declare Yourself, a nonpartisan youth voter initiative that has registered almost two million new young voters online in recent elections. The Declaration is still traveling. Declareyourself.com tells the full story.

In the truest sense, freedom cannot be bestowed; it must be achieved.

—FRANKLIN D. ROOSEVELT

When I turned eighty there was a big dinner in a prominent ballroom in Los Angeles where we raised a lot of money for People For the American Way. At the end of the evening I had the last word of course, and I found myself thanking eight hundred people or so who had attended and heard myself saying that I had something to confess to them. Even while I was speaking and expressing my gratitude, I found myself thinking of the taste of coffee the following morning—and that this evening was over. Then I said that perhaps the two least appreciated words in the English language were "over" and "next." This evening is over, I added, and I am already on to the next. As an afterthought, I commented that the hammock in the middle connecting over and next must be what they mean by "living in the moment." I've realized since that whatever I'm doing at the moment is what I'm deeply committed to, and that that is simply the center of my life.

The first time I ever thought about really being in the moment was when I came to know Jean Stapleton while producing *All in the Family.* I was asked what she was like, and I replied, "She's always where she is." I realized later that answer was really something important to strive for. It is so extraordinary to always be where you are. Wouldn't every child be so fortunate if they were raised by parents who were always *there* when they were with their children?

In the area of making a difference, life is like throwing a rock in the lake. If you throw a rock, a physicist might tell you, "Every time you throw a rock into the water, the level of the water rises." However, you turn to the physicist and say, "But I don't see it. I don't see the water rising." And the physicist would say, "The truth is you never get to see it, but you do see the ripple." That's the essence of pleasurable giving, being satisfied with the ripples.

When we've observed people touring and witnessing the Declaration of Independence when we've traveled the document around to people's hometowns, they have stood in a long line where they might even wait for an hour and a half to see it. I've seen teachers with tears in their eyes who have dreamed of taking their students to Washington to see such documents. "Now, right here in our town, the Declaration, I can't believe it!" I've heard them exclaim. And that's my ripple. Every downloaded voter registration form from Declareyourself.com is a ripple. Saying good morning to someone in a way that lifts them up and receiving them in a way that lifts you up is a ripple. We make a dent when we create those ripples. We all matter.

In the creator's great scheme of things, Earth being one planet among millions in a universe of which there are millions, how can you measure the distance between us or any of our accomplishments? We *all* matter. You can't get your thumb and forefinger close enough to measure the difference between the good any two of us can do—if you appreciate the vastness of the creator's enterprise here and our consequent insignificance. At the same time, how can we, each of us, open our eyes in the morning without recognizing that for each of us the world was created?

When I have been asked what writer has influenced me most, I'd answer, "Ralph Waldo Emerson on *Self-Reliance*. Everything I realize I've been saying is basically the lesson inherent in *Self-Reliance*." Someone had me wondering yesterday if our longevity didn't depend on how many people we touch, I mean really touch or inspire or impact every hour of our lives. Interesting to contemplate. Could be.

When it comes to giving, it's simple. We must give now. What immediately follows now is too late! Whenever I close any conversation I always say one thing.

"To be continued."

MAKE A DIFFERENCE TODAY

What are you doing that will "be continued?" Giving from the heart means moving toward a larger purpose. Do you have one? Do you want one? How could you get there from where you are today? Starting can be as simple as asking those closest to you to describe you—their insights may help you learn where you're headed as a giver. And do it now.

GIVING IS MUSIC TO HER EARS
Tena Clark, CEO, DMI Music & Media Solutions

DMIMusic.com

For the talented Tena Clark, the giving spirit shines through everything she does. Her attitude of gratitude and appreciation for her blessings is reflected in her service-driven life. As the Founder and Chief Executive of DMI Music & Media Solutions, Tena's company helps clients leverage the power of music and the unique sound at the heart of a successful brand. DMI has created musical brands and commercials for United Airlines, Subway Restaurants, McDonald's (she wrote the *Have You Had Your Break Today?* jingle), Target, Toyota, and Victoria's Secret, among many others. She also works with legendary talents like Natalie Cole and Aretha Franklin. Clark, an accomplished songwriter and producer, has created music for feature films and television shows including *My Best Friend's Wedding, Where the Heart Is, ER, Friends* and *Entertainment Tonight.* She wrote music and lyrics for Songs of Soul and Inspiration to mark AARP's fiftieth anniversary. She is co-Founder of Women of Grace, which provides scholarships that help low-income African-Americans in Clark's home state of Mississippi attend college.

We can only be said to be alive in those moments when our hearts are conscious of our treasures.

—THORNTON WILDER

I started playing the drums at age ten to help drown out some of the noise and chaos in my own life, and since that time I have always used music to express myself emotionally—both the pain and the joy. Life had gotten complicated at home in Waynesboro, a town of two thousand in rural Mississippi. Although our family was relatively well off, a divorce left my mom, Vera, with very few resources. It was my mom's choice, and it's one she made for her own happiness. I watched my mom through years of hardship, and I learned so much from her example. One of those things was the importance of tithing.

When her alimony reached the "princely sum" of $250 a month, Mom would sit down at the dining room table with her check book once a month. She would write out checks for one dollar each to twenty-five charities and people she wanted to help. No matter what, she would never miss a month because tithing 10 percent was what God taught, and that's all there was to it. I always thought this was a little crazy, but as I started to make a living I thought, "Maybe I should do this, too." But I wasn't serious—I'd pay for the mortgage and the groceries and other things, then I'd consider tithing based on 10 percent of what was left. I struggled with this until I heard God speaking to me. How dare I struggle with this when all of it belongs to God anyway! I was just blessed to have anything.

One of the biggest blessings of my life is the belief that if you give with the right spirit—from a place of no expectations—then your needs will somehow always be met. I also believe that the most valuable giving is giving when you don't think you have it to give. When you reach out on faith, it will come back to you!

MAKE A DIFFERENCE TODAY

Once you decide in your heart that it's important to give back, don't think you have to conquer the world or even change it. Let your heart and spirit lead. Find something you can do that will matter over time—like a drop of water on stone. Be confident that the blessings will come back, especially if you give when it's hardest.

GREAT ACTS OF PHILANTHROPY
Marc Pollick, Founder and President,
The Giving Back Fund

Givingback.org

Marc Pollick, President and Founder of The Giving Back Fund, formulated the idea for an organization that would work with celebrities to leverage their fame and wealth for the common good. The Giving Back Fund was established in 1997 to provide philanthropic management and consulting services to professional athletes, entertainers, business entrepreneurs, and others. His idea—to harness wealth and celebrity and leverage both on behalf of philanthropy—has resulted in a dynamic, collaborative, high profile community of giving. The Giving Back Fund has a mission of "Integrity and Innovation in Philanthropy." Examples are called "Great Acts of Philanthropy."

Prior to establishing The Giving Back Fund, Marc worked for many years with Elie Wiesel, author, Holocaust survivor, and winner of the Nobel Peace Prize. Marc later created a foundation in Elie's name to institutionalize his work in human rights around the world. While working at the Elie Wiesel Foundation, Marc began to realize the power of celebrity to do good, and that the spotlight that shines on a celebrity could be redirected instead on an important cause and mission. Professional athletes and entertainers have distinct privileges that their celebrity confer including wealth, a fan base, team relationships, and media exposure. Marc believed that using these attributes effectively and thoughtfully on behalf of philanthropy would create a powerful "giving juggernaut." In just eleven years, The Giving Back Fund has created charitable foundations for more than seventy-five celebrities including Yao Ming, Jamie Lynn Sigler, Nancy Kerrigan, Jalen Rose, Shawn Marion, Elton Brand, Shane Battier, Ben Roethlisberger, and La' Roi Glover, among many others.

No one has ever become poor by giving.

—ANNE FRANK

The Giving Back Fund's vision is, "A society in which becoming a successful philanthropist is as valued and desirable a goal as success in athletics, business, entertainment, or any other field." The opportunity to help others drives my passion and purpose for success. Many philanthropists are beginning to live that mission, and society is witnessing philanthropists give their money away in ever increasing numbers and amounts. The power to leverage celebrity on behalf of philanthropy is the essence of The Giving Back Fund.

Despite their inconsistencies, celebrities are still viewed as role models in society, so why not use celebrity for good? Many celebrities, such as Andre Agassi and Angelina Jolie, have used their status and fame to give back to the community in powerful and creative ways.

Bill Gates and Warren Buffett know they can give half of their fortune to good use and in addition give their own time and commitment to enriching the lives of others. Paul Newman established his philanthropic legacy with Newman's Own. At first, Paul had anticipated minimum sales, but in less than three decades $200 million has been given to charity through Newman's Own proceeds. In collaboration with leading business schools around the country, The Giving Back Fund is preparing unique case studies on the history of the most successful celebrity philanthropists. The Fund will make these case histories about best practices in celebrity philanthropy available online to help guide up-and-coming celebrity philanthropists as well as others in the philanthropic, sports, and entertainment communities.

Basketball legend Michael Jordan closed his own foundation because of difficulties in administering it. Professional management and oversight of celebrity foundations is imperative if they are to have maximum impact. The Fund guarantees that its non-charitable overhead will be no higher than 5 percent for the minimum donation of $250,000, down to 1 percent for a $5 million gift.

The Giving Back Fund is creating a program called The American Philanthropy Hall of Fame, where extraordinary acts of philanthropy across ten categories will be modeled on an annual basis on national television around Thanksgiving. These inspirational stories exemplify the goodwill and spirit of America and explain why philanthropy is uniquely interwoven into the fabric of our society.

During a White House Conference on Philanthropy, then First Lady Hillary Clinton shared that if we just increased our annual contributions to charity a tiny percentage it could have a huge impact nationwide. People aspire to go to the moon. They can all give back.

The Fund teamed up with NBA Superstar Yao Ming of the Houston Rockets. In response to the recent earthquake disaster in China, we created a game plan for rebuilding almost two hundred schools. A $2 million gift from Yao Ming generated almost $4 million of other donations in just three short weeks. Yao's donation, recognizable status, and public persona have spurred others to contribute to his worthy cause. This is the spirit of The Giving Back Fund—to harness celebrity power for the common philanthropic good.

Make a Difference Today

Challenge your friends and associates around a purposeful act of giving—local or beyond. Consider getting a local celebrity to work with you to give your cause visibility and increase donations. You can partner with a local nonprofit or go it alone. You'll be surprised at how accessible some celebrities are and what a boost their participation will give your effort.

A Leader for a Lifetime
Dr. Dorothy Height, Chair and President Emerita, National Council of Negro Women

Dream giver and earth shaker, Dr. Dorothy Height has followed and expanded on the original purpose of the National Council of Negro Women, giving new meaning, new courage, and pride to women, youth, and families everywhere. Throughout her career, she has been a leader in the struggle for equality and human rights for all people. Her life exemplifies her passionate commitment for a just society and her vision of a better world. Born in 1912, she is one of the oldest living civil rights leaders.

> *Life's most persistent and urgent question is: what are you doing for others?*

> —Martin Luther King Jr.

I grew up seeing my mother helping others, and I have always enjoyed giving. Even before my teen years, I was always making things for people. I made paper flowers for sick people and was always looking out for others. That was something I just did on my own. When I was fourteen, I entered an oration contest sponsored by the Elks. It was on the Constitution of the United States, and I wrote an oration and focused on the thirteenth, fourteenth and fifteenth amendments. I was so intrigued by it and won the contest! The prize was a four-year scholarship to college at New York University.

As a teenager, studying the fourteenth amendment was especially important to me, and I became very active. I became the Vice Chair of the United Christian Youth Movement of North America. That experience with other young people kindled my interest in justice issues and the economic order, and I just kept going from there.

I'm proud that I had the chance to work with other civil rights leaders. When I first met Dr. Martin Luther King, he was fifteen years old, and he came to Morehouse College as a gifted student. Ten years later when Rosa Parks took her stand and wouldn't give up her seat on the bus, Dr. King rose to leadership, and for me it was quite an experience working along with him and the United Civil Rights Leadership Movement. This was a group that planned the strategies for civil rights. Working with Dr. King and other civil rights leaders gave me a sense of what we had to do in the present and the future.

The next generation needs to know that you cannot be yourself and at your best if you are interested only in yourself. We have to start early and help children learn how to share, and give them a sense of feeling responsible for other people. Little children have to learn how to work together. We are confronted with a generation that often thinks first about themselves as individuals. I am pleased with the progress that has been made, but I cannot be happy until we have fulfilled the obligations we have and the roles to make freedom possible.

Working with others helps you to grow. I have learned not just from great people but also from working with people whose names may never be known. You learn to work with them, and you learn more about yourself and the strength in yourself and service to others. I would hope that young people would understand that it's not about things, it's about relationships and the relationship that we have with each other that we are all related to each other and we must work with each other and make our period of life better. Giving is sharing, and giving is a channel through which you do for others, and whether you realize it or not you are also helping yourself.

I live with a sense that there's a purpose for my life and that God didn't just put me here, but there's a purpose and I'm driven by my sense of purpose. Giving matters because it's an expression of caring, and we all need to care more not just about our own children, but all children, not just about ourselves, but others, and care more not just about our own country or our own community but the world in which we live. We can make this a better place for everyone, a place where equality is more than a slogan.

I learned from Rosa Parks what it means to give and to serve without worrying about who will get the credit, to do what your heart and mind moves you with a sense of purpose to do. Rosa was one of my heroes. Rosa is an example of how one person acting on a base of faith and determination can make a difference.

Make a Difference Today

It is important to understand that when we give we ultimately help ourselves understand a richer, purposeful way of living. Begin by thinking of needs in your community. Is there an organization that could benefit by your time or energy? What might you do for a neighbor in need?

Building a Field of Dreams for Golfers
Renee Powell, LPGA/PGA Golf Professional, Clearview Golf Course

Clearview-GC.com

Professional golfer and educator Renee Powell is one of only three African-American women to ever play on the Ladies Professional Golf Association's (LPGA) Tour. Powell was inspired to play by her legendary father, William Powell, owner of the Clearview Golf Course in East Canton, Ohio. Her father was the first African American to design and own a golf course. After World War II, her father couldn't find a course that would let African Americans play, so he dedicated his life to building one and, in that way, to fighting discrimination.

Renee began competing as a golfer at age twelve and made her professional debut on the LPGA Tour in 1967. Her first tournament was the U.S. Women's Open conducted by the United States Golf Association. After completing the tour in 1980, she taught golf in Europe and Africa and returned home, where she currently serves as the head professional golfer at her father's legendary course. In 2001, the Clearview Golf Course was named to the National Register of Historic Places, and the Powell family established the Clearview Legacy Foundation for education, preservation, and research. In 2003, Renee Powell received the First Lady of Golf Award from the Professional Golfers' Association. In 2007 she was the recipient of the first For the Love of the Game award by Rolex, and in 2008 received an honorary Doctor of Laws degree from the University of St. Andrews in Scotland. Renee was the third American to receive this distinguished award.

We ask for nothing special. We ask only to be permitted to live as you live, and as our nation's Constitution provides.

—JACKIE ROBINSON

My father was a proud World War II veteran who had fought for his country in a then-segregated Army. But he was not allowed to play golf on any course here when he returned from overseas. During his service, he had been welcomed at golf courses in Scotland and England and passionately loved the game. Dad, who had begun to play golf at age nine, thought things would be better at home. But they weren't. So he decided to find a way to build a course in his home state of Ohio where everyone would be welcome. My father had taught two black doctors to play golf and talked them both into joining him in investing in his dream. He borrowed his portion, and began building the course with his own hands.

The property was a rundown dairy farm filled with fence posts and trees which my father cleared with a tractor and borrowed equipment. He plowed the land and seeded the course by hand— all while maintaining a full-time job in order to support his family. It took less than two years, and the course opened to the public in 1948. There weren't many golf courses in the area, and about 95 percent of our clientele was white, but he was determined to spread his love of the game to everyone.

I admire the many lessons my parents taught me. They achieved so much with so little and so little recognition. I started playing golf when I was three years old. I learned to walk, talk, and play golf; it was second nature. Now, I'm the head golf professional at the course. My brother is the course superintendent and is in charge of grounds maintenance. From being thrown into all of this, I've grown as a person. We created the Clearview Legacy Foundation in 2001 for education, preservation, and research. The Foundation uses golf as a tool to help others, especially young people, become better citizens in the areas of vocation and education.

I've just found golf to be such a peaceful pursuit and a way to build confidence and self-esteem. In the '80s I'll never forget when I taught young girls in Africa to play. Upon a return visit, I ended up on a team playing the President of Zambia with some of the ladies I had taught. One woman hugged me and cried, telling me she never thought she'd meet her President, and now she was playing golf with him!

We all inhabit one earth. God has put us here not to be selfish, but to embrace others and make this world a better world. To help those who are struggling to find their purpose in life. This is what we are meant to do. The world can only be better if we help each other. Some may bury their talents, while others spread and grow them to make a better life for others. My family has given everything they have to keeping this golf course alive, and it remains our mission to make golf a sport that is available to everyone.

MAKE A DIFFERENCE TODAY

When you share your passion for a particular skill or talent that you have, you share yourself in a meaningful way that lets everyone shine. Giving of your time and talents is a way to give a new purpose to someone else. By helping another person learn how to do something new, you will discover that one of the greatest presents is to share the gift of your presence and your skills.

SHARING LIFE'S GOLDEN TICKET
Brendon Burchard, CEO and Founder,
The Burchard Group LLC

BrendonBurchard.com

Brendon Burchard, author of *Life's Golden Ticket*, is an acclaimed leadership speaker and business consultant. He is revolutionizing the way authors, speakers, and entrepreneurs do business by teaching them to partner with major nonprofits and Fortune 500 companies. Burchard was blessed to receive life's golden ticket— a second chance—ten years ago after surviving a dramatic car accident in a third-world country. Since then, he has dedicated his life to helping individuals, teams, and organizations create and master change for the betterment of all people.

Our opportunities to do good are our talents.

—COTTON MATHER

A decade ago I survived a dramatic car accident in a third-world country. To this day, I vividly remember the moment I pulled myself free from the twisted metal of the wreckage. I escaped the car through the shattered windshield, and remember feeling the life draining out of me and thinking, "Did I live?" I wondered if there was a purpose to life, if there had been a reason I was here. When I looked up and saw this great big beautiful moon in the sky, I realized I was still alive. I felt as if as if the Big Guy above had reached down and handed me life's golden ticket—a second chance at life. It was like, "Here you go kid, you get another shot at this, now go out and make a difference and do it fast because now you know the clock is ticking."

From that day forward, I've worked every day to earn my second chance. There's not a night that goes by that I don't wonder aloud, "Did I matter today? Did I make a difference?" It's in this spirit that I make all my decisions. It's from this sense of meaning that I've created some of the largest nonprofit partnerships in history, joined so many nonprofit boards, volunteered so many hours, and used my business, skills, talents, and blessings to do good in the world while doing good in business.

I discovered that many of the nonprofit organizations I worked with or contributed to didn't know about or pursue relationships with organizations across the street or across the nation that basically served the same demographic. And I found out that most Fortune 500 companies didn't have a clue about many of the nonprofits making a difference in their backyards. So, I created the Global Partnership Summit to bring together the world's Fortune 500 senior executives, nonprofit leaders, global foundation leaders, and social entrepreneurs to learn about each other and work together to address the greatest problems of our times. I figured if they could team up and truly leverage one another's infrastructure and resources to make a difference—to go beyond "cause marketing" to truly solving problems together—then we could change the world on a massive scale.

MAKE A DIFFERENCE TODAY

As individuals, we face daily choices. We can either let society exist as it does, with so many people lost and forgotten, or we can choose to light this world with the sunshine of service. It's a matter of coming together with the common purpose of protecting and enhancing our humanity. We can make change, but we must work together and continually ask now, not in the twilight of our lives but *now*, "Do I matter?"

CHAPTER 2

Redefining Giving

S ome inspiring and accomplished people are redefining giving and the way we think about it. Call them trailblazers or mavericks. They are teaching us the core values of giving and showing us that there's something more important going on that transforms the undercurrent of what people really need. As we add our own imprint to the world of important causes, we also add to the new forefront of giving. Each of us can make a difference, and it's a collective understanding that strengthens the byproducts of our efforts.

As you read the following stories, you'll be amazed by the unique approaches of a selection of leading-edge givers, by their energy, persistence, and creativity. When they encounter an obstacle to their goal, they think of new approaches. When the old way no longer works, they find a new way. They are solution architects. People who are less committed sometimes use an obstacle as an excuse to abandon a goal. As we spoke to the leaders in this chapter, we were inspired by their examples not only of fortitude but of extreme creativity.

In Chapter One, we discussed finding ways to use your personal skills to give, and these people have the ability to solve problems. If you have a background in finding solutions for businesses or organizations, if you're a can-do manager who finds a way to get things done no matter what challenges you face, use the examples of the people in this chapter to inspire you to apply your skills to giving. There are many organizations near you who can benefit from the skills you bring to their causes. As we've said elsewhere in this book, you don't need to have financial resources to give. You can make a difference with your time and talents.

Most of all, the people in this chapter don't give up. They seek innovative ideas and new ways of doing things to improve the lives of people in need. And you'll notice that achieving the goal gives them great happiness, a sense of fulfillment they have not found in any other pursuit. These resourceful people obviously love what they do. By giving, they receive.

It Starts with the Heart
Barbara J. Krumsiek, CEO and President,
The Calvert Group, Ltd.

Calvert.com

Calvert Group was one of the first companies to formally oppose apartheid in South Africa by divesting of companies doing business there in the 1980s. A leading investment management and mutual fund firm, Calvert is headquartered in Bethesda, Maryland. The company manages approximately $16 billion in assets across forty-one mutual funds, including a number of funds with sustainable and responsible investment practices and an emphasis on community investing. Since 1997, social activist Barbara Krumsiek has led Calvert and overseen a period of dramatic growth and increased visibility, especially within socially responsible investments. Her career in the investment sector spans three decades. Prior to joining Calvert Group, Krumsiek was a Managing Director at Alliance Capital Management LP in New York City. Krumsiek is responsible for development of the Calvert Women's Principles, a code of corporate conduct focusing on gender equality and women's empowerment. She has also been a champion of efforts to achieve diversity in corporate boardrooms. Her business success and activism have led to many honors and awards, including being named by *Washingtonian Magazine* as one of the "150 Most Influential People in Washington, D.C." In 2008,

Krumsiek received the CEO Leadership Award from *Washington Business Journal* and Greater D.C. Cares.

No act of kindness, no matter how small, is ever wasted.

—AESOP

One of the most exciting moments for me was a call I got a number of years ago while I was doing some volunteering in downtown Washington, D.C. It was a member of my staff calling with great excitement to say that Zanele Mbeki, wife of Thabo Mvuyelwa Mbeki, the second President of post-apartheid South Africa, was on her way to our office! She was on her first state visit to the United States, and she wanted to visit Calvert to learn more about socially responsible investment practices. Mrs. Mbeki had a state dinner to attend that night, but felt it was important to visit and meet with us in person. It was a huge tribute to Calvert and the rich heritage of social justice that was established long before I arrived.

When it comes to corporate philanthropy, you have to start with the heart. It's not about just figuring out where the dollars get spent, which is the traditional thinking. It's about starting at the place where you're drawn to make a difference. Calvert is the sum of its parts, and as well as offering socially conscious investment opportunities we create an environment for engagement and giving for all of our associates. One way we do that is by giving everyone a paid day of leave once a month which is not tied to vacation. The volunteer activity is the associate's choice. Some read to children, some get involved in projects like Habitat for Humanity, and many participate in a wonderful program called Food and Friends, which delivers meals to the home-bound elderly and AIDS patients. Not long ago our entire legal department shut down for a day so that associates could build for Habitat. It was wonderful to see our hardworking lawyers hammering away in hard hats. They were out of their element but they were contributing a great deal! We've found that these kinds of opportunities add to our associates' productivity and sense of overall well-being. A volunteerism policy like ours is good for many things, including the bottom line.

There's a real sense of engagement by everyone here, and we like to recognize it. To me, a company is known for the kind of behavior it rewards. Every year we give an award to an associate who has done significant work in community volunteerism. It's a much-coveted award, and we applaud its recipient loud and long. One of our recent winners was a research analyst whose wife is in the military. Through her, he became aware of the needs and organized a major drive for Christmas gifts for the families of returning, injured military people. Another winner is one of our portfolio managers, a former teacher who established a personal scholarship fund to help low-income students attend private schools. I feel that Calvert is the kind of place where you can be a whole person—it's not about checking your identity at the door and forgetting the issues you care about. For me one of those issues is women's leadership and involvement in politics and business.

MAKE A DIFFERENCE TODAY

If your place of work does not have a volunteerism policy, talk to your human resources director about the possibility. Volunteer to head an employee committee to research the idea and prepare a proposal. These policies address everything from time off of work for community outreach to matching gifts for charities and one-time special needs during global crises.

Rise Above. Give Back.

Jerry White, Executive Director, Survivor Corps

SurvivorCorps.org

Jerry White's life changed forever in 1984 when he lost his leg in a landmine explosion while visiting Israel. The experience motivated him to become a leader in the International Campaign to Ban Landmines, co-recipient of the 1997 Nobel Prize for Peace. Today, White's focus has moved beyond landmines to touch the lives of people affected in diverse ways by global conflict. He founded the remarkable organization Survivor Corps, a global network of people helping one another overcome the pain of war and contribute to society. Its premise is that giving back is the ultimate means to healing. The organization has taken the lead in establishing international standards for survivor and disability rights around the world. In just over a decade, Survivor Corps (and its predecessor, Landmine Survivors Network) has made enormous contributions, drafting and negotiating landmark human rights treaties including the U.N. Convention on the Rights of People with Disabilities. In his book, *I Will Not Be Broken*, Jerry White examined the lives of thousands of survivors and wrote about the five steps to overcoming a life crisis. Most important for healing, he concluded, is being able to reach out to someone else.

> *Together, we are not alone. Together, we can be more. Together, we survive and thrive.*

> —Survivor Corps credo

How do some people not only survive "explosive moments" in their lives, but grow stronger and thrive, while others remain stuck in their misfortunes, unable to move forward in the face of personal tragedy? It's one of the key questions I asked thousands of survivors for my book. We talked to survivors of cancer, landmine explosions, rape and incest, addiction, miscarriage, and even the Holocaust. Their unforgettable stories helped me identify the following steps:

Face facts. Recognize that this awful thing has happened and you can't turn back the clock.

Choose life, not death. Remember that finding a better future is a daily choice.

Reach out. You need to let people into your life to support you in a crisis.

Get moving. Understand that suffering has come your way, and it's time to get off the couch and into action. You have to do your own "survivor sit-ups"—no one can do the rehab but you.

Give back. What we learned about giving back was really the frosting on the survivorship cake! Those who were able to give in small and large ways in the course of their recovery went beyond just recovering. As a result of giving back they grew stronger and found meaning in life after their explosive moments.

Ramiz is a landmine survivor we helped in Bosnia. When we met him he had lost a leg *and* lost his place in society. Depressed and out of work, he moved in with his in-laws and started drinking too much. Once he joined our outreach network in Bosnia, things started to turn around. Ramiz faced the facts of his life, was able to get a new fake leg, and began work on a business plan for raising and selling vegetables. We helped him get a greenhouse, tools, and support to jumpstart his vegetable-growing business. One thing we require of everyone in our program is community service—the giving back piece. Ramiz vividly remembers the time he was first able to donate more than four hundred pounds of tomatoes to a local orphanage. It was an incredible giveback moment for him, and he told us about it with a glowing smile. Now he was no longer the beneficiary but the benefactor. Ramiz even trained to become one of our survivor leaders in fifty countries. We send outreach workers like him, who are themselves survivors, to the front lines of a global crisis. Or, in the case of survivors in Vietnam, it may be years after the crisis before we are led to work toward recovery. The work is especially important in countries with few doctors or psychiatrists, because these survivor mentors become lifelines and role models for change.

Giving is the key. Even though victims can't imagine having an ounce of anything inside them to give, the mystery is that once they find that ounce, all they want is to give more. Survivors who have felt the sting of war and other crises are standing up together and saying, "No more." For us, this survivor movement is really a peace movement. We've taken our injuries in hand and advocated for global change—from a ban on landmines in 1997 to the recent ban on cluster munitions in 2008. In the end, our tag line says it all: *Rise above. Give back.*

Make a Difference Today

When it seems the hardest thing in the world to do, consider reaching out to someone else. If you've lost a loved one, suffered an injury or been tossed around by life, consider how you might benefit by finding someone to help through their pain. It's very hard to take that first step. Try to do it and see what happens.

GIVING IT ALL IN LIFE'S SECOND HALF
Marc Freedman, Founder and CEO, Civic Ventures

Encore.org

Civic Ventures is a dynamic think tank on boomers, aging, and work founded and led by Marc Freedman. As Chief Executive Officer, Freedman leads the movement for millions of Americans, encouraging baby boomers who finish their midlife careers to find encore careers that serve the public good. Freedman's book, *Encore: Finding Work That Matters in the Second Half of Life*, sets the message for Civic Ventures: Now is the time for millions of baby boomers to become a vital workforce for social change.

Every day, over ten thousand new baby boomers are added to the population. Funneling this human talent into service is vital to the welfare of our nation and to the lives of the individuals themselves. Civic Ventures CEO Marc Freedman works to define the second half of adult life as a time of individual and social renewal.

The years teach much which the days never knew.

—RALPH WALDO EMERSON

For half a century, marketers and developers sold the Golden Years ideal of freedom *from* work. But today few want to be on the sidelines for thirty years—and hardly anyone can afford it. Instead they want the freedom *to* work in new ways and to new and more important ends.

Civic Ventures demonstrates the value of experience in solving serious social problems and works as a catalyst to spur individual and organizational action. Boomers want to keep contributing and make the country a better place. The challenge of *practical idealism* is to turn the push into a pull where people actually look forward to being a part of a social movement that has a sense of purpose. The compelling vision for a longer, more fulfilling life surely makes a virtue out of a necessity.

The Network: The hub of the Civic Ventures campaign is *Encore. org*, a growing resource for and network of people who want work that matters in the second half of life.

The Research: Civic Ventures regularly works with researchers and polling firms to assess attitudes about retirement and work. New surveys show that half of all Americans age fifty to seventy want work that helps others. A full 50 percent are interested in taking jobs now and in retirement that help improve quality of life in their communities. They want good jobs in education and social services, health care, and government.

The Entrepreneurs: Civic Ventures' Purpose Prize provides $100,000 awards to social innovators over sixty who have created new ways to solve some of the world's biggest problems. The Purpose Prize is awarded to individuals who discover new opportunities, invent new programs and foster lasting social change.

The Organizations: Civic Ventures created the The BreakThrough Award to identify and recruit innovative organizations that exemplify the passion and experience of people over fifty to address societal needs. The program salutes nonprofit or public service agencies that engage their workforces for good.

The Mentors: Civic Ventures runs Experience Corps, a program engaging people over fifty-five as tutors and mentors in urban public schools. Today, more than two thousand older adults work as Experience Corps members, helping twenty thousand young students in more than twenty cities who are struggling to learn to read.

The Paths: Civic Ventures encourages community colleges to help prepare boomers for encore careers through its Encore Community College Grants Program. Grants have been awarded to ten innovative community colleges that are creating new ways for adults fifty-plus to transition to "encore careers" in education, health care, and social services—all sectors facing critical labor shortages.

Today America can forge a new and compelling vision of the second half of life: One that revolves around work, purpose, and meaning. One that solves social problems instead of creating them.

Through strategic investments in powerful ideas, Civic Ventures is leading the way to a society that makes more sense—for everyone.

MAKE A DIFFERENCE TODAY

Unsung heroes can be recognized in so many meaningful ways. While these dedicated souls do not volunteer or give of themselves for recognition, when we praise others it spreads the word about everyday people doing kind things and inspires us all to follow in their footsteps. Show an attitude of gratitude to others for the work they do and recognize the power of your praise and appreciation. Kindness is contagious.

THE FREEDOM TO CARE
Eva Haller, Philanthropist, Activist, and Free the Children USA Board Chair

FreetheChildren.org

As a child living in occupied Hungary, Eva Haller followed her older brother underground into the resistance. Under cover of darkness they worked to print and distribute anti-Nazi leaflets. She eventually went into hiding, and although she lost her beloved brother, she saved her own life by bravely facing down a German policeman. After the war, Haller made her way to the United States, where she cleaned houses and went to school at night, eventually becoming a New York City social worker. She and her late husband Murray Roman became successful business owners, but they wanted more out of life than commercial success. They decided to spend a year working abroad for UNICEF and never stopped giving. After Murray's death, Eva was fortunate to meet and marry a physician, Yoel Haller, who shares her passion and dedication to help those less fortunate who are in need. She is the Chair of the board of Free the Children USA, a network of children helping children to end poverty and exploitation in forty-five countries. She also works tirelessly on behalf of women in developing nations and is a longtime environmental advocate. For Haller, personal philanthropy is a way of celebrating the life and freedom she cherishes.

Never believe that a few caring people can't change the world.

For, indeed, that's all who ever have.

—MARGARET MEAD

I work on behalf of the oppressed because I experienced oppression. My experiences during World War II and afterwards in the civil rights and women's movements helped me see that so many of the best and brightest ideas come from young people. They have hope and energy, and they just refuse to believe that something is impossible! This to me is a special spiritual quality. But it's not about religion; it's more about a way of looking at the world—a fundamental belief in the power of change.

That quality—that belief—is why I work for Free the Children. We must recognize and foster the special power and initiative of the young. Through our programs, more than a million young people have been involved in youth-led fundraising and programs like Halloween for Hunger and Adopt a Village. Free the Children has built more than five hundred primary schools in developing countries. We help improve the lives of children so that they're well fed, don't have to work, and can attend school ready to learn. And we encourage young men and women here in North America to become change makers.

The eldest five of our fourteen grandchildren have spent their summers building schools in Africa, South America, India, and

Thailand. We want them to see what it means to build with their own hands. My life has always been a response to perceived need. When people tell me that I'm "giving back" I tell them they're wrong. Every time we give, we give to ourselves.

MAKE A DIFFERENCE TODAY

Children raise chickens and send their egg money to Free the Children to help build schools. In wedding invitations, donations to charities are requested instead of wedding presents. Rather than tangible gifts, consider giving donations this holiday season. You'll reduce your carbon footprint, spend a lot less in postage, and give the recipient something of unique value.

Finding Your Cathedral
Bill Shore, Founder and Executive Director,
Share Our Strength

Strength.org

Bill Shore founded Share Our Strength in 1984 in response to the Ethiopian famine and subsequently renewed concern about hunger in the United States. Share Our Strength is now the leading organization working to end childhood hunger in the United States. Since its founding, Share Our Strength has raised more than $200 million to support more than a thousand of the most effective hunger-relief organizations around the globe. Today, its priority is to end childhood hunger in America ensuring that the more than twelve million American children at risk of hunger have access to the nutritious food they need to learn, grow, and thrive.

> *What do we live for, if it is not to make life less difficult for each other?*

> —George Elliot

The most important thing to consider when it comes to giving is to find a way to give that represents your unique talents and gifts. Most people discover their unique value when they give something that somehow represents who they are. What they give reflects their skills, talents, or interests, and it's the kind of giving that doesn't lead to "giving burn out." There's a lot of talk of "compassion fatigue" because people who are giving donate or get engaged in multiple community endeavors, but when you are sharing your own gifts and talents—like chefs teaching low-income families to cook—you give in a way that moves people and helps people bridge the divide. That is the most meaningful way you can give.

A young man named Zach Steinberg went to Ethiopia as part of a group of young people while he was a medical student at George Washington University in Washington, D.C. Upon his return, with Share Our Strength's support he organized other medical students to use their talents by returning to Africa and volunteering their time to provide medical services at Ethiopian clinics and hospitals. In this example, Zach recognized the needs of a community and immediately took action to share his strength and his knowledge of medicine.

The landscape of giving is changing, and there's a real convergence of forces taking place around entrepreneurs. The forces of philanthropy cause us to search for ideas and find more innovative ways to impact others, and that's a good thing. It suggests that the way we've done things is not a justification for doing things the same way. We must explore and experiment in new ways.

We give for reasons of compassion and concern. In the face of Hurricane Katrina and the tsunami, people gave in generous ways that were unprecedented. The most important thing in my life has been being a good father, and giving starts at home. I have three children, and of everything I do what I hope for the most is that I've inspired them to give generously to the next generation.

Unfortunately, in giving the trend is to treat the symptoms of issues rather than the underlying causes. In the case of Share Our Strength, a lot of people want to give food to provide to the hungry, which is compassionate and important, but they are not dedicated to the root cause of hunger, which is poverty. People must be willing to give without always seeing the end results of their efforts.

I wrote a book titled *The Cathedral Within* (Random House, 1999), and the main concept of the book summarizes this idea. The most important ethic of the cathedral builders is that they knew they couldn't see their hard work finished, yet they did the work because they were inspired and it was the right thing to do. It took up to five hundred years to finish one cathedral in Milan.

Make a Difference Today

It's important to understand the definition of strength. It is defined as talent or skill that you already possess. When you give of your strength, you are offering something that embodies your spirit and the essence of who you are. When you align your strengths and these abilities with a cause or person who can benefit from them, you create a deeper connection.

COOKIN' UP CHANGE
Robert Egger, President, D.C. Central Kitchen

DCCentralKitchen.org

Robert Egger—also known as Mr. Robert—founded the D.C. Central Kitchen in 1989. He is also a leader of the Nonprofit Congress and the author of *Begging For Change: The Dollars and Sense of Making Nonprofits Responsive, Efficient, and Rewarding for All (HarperCollins with Howard Yoon)*. His nonprofit organization is considered a national model of charity and efficiency in two ways: first, the staff collects unserved food that would be otherwise discarded by hotels, restaurants, and corporate cafeterias in the community. Second, homeless people, ex-cons, and others prepare four thousand meals a day for the needy. They are each enrolled in a twelve-week job-training program and work with chefs. Volunteers from all over the Washington area come to help, but leave knowing that the act of giving is in everyone helping.

> *The luxury of doing good surpasses every other personal enjoyment.*
>
> —JOHN GAY

Giving feels great. Sometimes we think it's supposed to be ashes and sackcloth, and we are not supposed to enjoy this and feel sorry for people, but that is not accurate. Giving is the most enjoyable thing in the world. The spiritual exercise you get when you give is incredible. I'm forty-eight and might be a little soft, but my soul is buffed. If you want to find happiness, go out and give.

The secret to giving is that next time you go looking for your heart's content, you won't have to look any farther than your back yard. That's the secret. Don't think you have to go across town. Often it's your friend or your next-door neighbor. Start local. When I get calls and people ask if they can help feed the homeless, I send them to a senior center or retirement home and tell them just to visit. Take your kid, your dog, some plants, and just visit.

Everybody can give. Everybody has a role. For example, here at the D.C. Kitchen, everyday someone helps someone. High school students are working next to men and women. We are in our sixty-seventh job training. Together they are preparing four thousand meals, and while they do that they will also have—without anyone telling them—innocent discussions. Over the course of three or four hours, I guarantee those men and women will develop a bond with these students, and both will realize that we accomplished something and stood next to someone who was different. These men and women coming through here are considered the bottom of society, but they get into our program, and I pray we are raising this younger generation to come along with new breakthroughs.

There was this one little girl. She and her family made a difference by making sandwiches every week. There's a group of kids in an afternoon program, and now they get a snack. These sandwiches allow their mothers to focus on their new jobs because they know their kids have a snack and it's a safe place to go. At that same place, there's another younger or older person mentoring that child. When they go there, their little engines are recharged and so they can process their homework. It's all about one person visiting and mentoring and another person making one sandwich and then a mother knowing she can focus on her job and maybe get a raise. That one sandwich made all these people profoundly happy.

The most important thing the D.C. Central Kitchen has accomplished is to elevate understanding about the potential everybody has to contribute. Most people think that charity is giving, but it's really about giving to people so that everybody has something to contribute. I did a speech recently and said if we get down to it, we have tried everything, but working together is all that's left. Everybody has something to contribute, but a lot of what we do is all wrapped up in the redemption of the giver, not the liberation of the receiver, and we have to reverse that.

We also have to have discussions about the issues. We have to have dialogue. I speak a lot on change, and I discovered that once you get past the comfort zones change is stifled by fear. Most people are generous in America, but they are afraid of conversations about domestic violence and race issues, so we pretend. Feeding people is decent but won't solve the hunger. Only purposeful and uncomfortable discussions will make change. The answer to hunger in America is not more D.C. Central Kitchens but a real solid discussion about the issue of hunger.

Another important issue is the economics of giving. Nonprofits are built on extra money, time, and food, and what happens when and if there's no extra? Look at the economics of America and the world economy. We can't keep charity supported forever. Either we have a discussion on systematic solutions, or we run the risk of the economy tanking.

As we redefine giving, we have huge opportunities and are making breakthroughs. Today's nonprofit world isn't about charity, and its leaders mean business. Nonprofits must stop chasing money and start focusing on the true work at hand. In business, you can profit by doing the right thing, and that's not bad. One of the things that interest me as boomers age is that they have more money and freedom than anyone else in history. Did we use it the way we should have? There's a new opportunity in America to redefine what is a life well lived.

MAKE A DIFFERENCE TODAY

When you are looking for ways to give, look around you. Start local. Small steps can lead to big changes in the lives of those in need and in your own life. Begin by asking people you come in contact with today if there's someone they know who needs a little help. Ask is there anything you can do? Select one small generous deed you can do today and like Nike says, "Just do it!"

GIVING THE GIFT OF AN OPEN MIND
Dr. Georgette Bennett, President and Founder,
Tanenbaum Center for Interreligious Understanding

Tanenbaum.org

Promoting peace and overcoming religious intolerance is the work of the Tanenbaum Center for Interreligious Understanding, a nonsectarian organization that does its urgently needed work in schools, workplaces, and areas of armed conflict. The Center was founded by Dr. Georgette Bennett to build on the work of her late husband, Rabbi Marc Tanenbaum, world-renowned human rights and social justice activist and pioneer in the field of interreligious reconciliation. The son of immigrants, Rabbi Tanenbaum was known as the father of Jewish-Christian relations, but in his career he reached out to all religions. He attended the Second Vatican Council in 1965 and helped draft *Nostra Aetate*, which decreed that Catholics could not blame Jews for the death of Jesus. The document helped heal the rift between the two faiths. After Rabbi Tanenbaum's untimely death in 1992, Dr. Bennett started the Center. It focuses on three areas: religion and diversity education, religious diversity in the workplace, and religion and conflict resolution.

> *Ultimately, America's answer to the intolerant man is diversity, the very diversity which our heritage of religious freedom has inspired.*

> —ROBERT F. KENNEDY

I was born in Budapest to Holocaust survivors. In 1948, our family escaped from Hungary and settled in France for about five years while waiting for our U.S. visas. We arrived here in 1952, and my father died soon after. This was the end of the McCarthy era, and having come from a Communist country, the witch-hunt environment left my mother very afraid and had a profound impact on me as well. We had lost 120 members of our family in the Holocaust, after which my parents faced Communist oppression in Hungary. I came to understand that the civil rights that are the undergirding of this country are the most American thing we have.

I attended Vassar College and then went on to get a Ph.D. in sociology from NYU. After a period of teaching sociology and criminology, I convinced a local television news director that I should work as a consultant and reporter. Eventually I became a network correspondent for NBC News, and spent about ten years working all over the dial in broadcast journalism. I married Marc in the middle of my broadcasting career; when he died I was eight months pregnant with our only child. Two weeks after his death, I got a call from the head of the International Council of Christians and Jews who said, "Georgette, we must do something to continue Marc's work, because people so quickly forget." Compared to my parents' suffering, I had led a life of extraordinary privilege, and this was an opportunity for me to give back.

We incorporated the Center at the end of 1992 and started operating in 1993. Our goal was to go beyond dialogue and establish on-the-ground programs that could reach broad audiences. We've done that, for example, by producing an interactive tool kit to help managers deal with religious differences in the workplace. We help corporations create policy and develop interventions when conflicts arise. As well, the Center supports peacemakers in areas of armed conflict. In Nigeria, an imam and a pastor who were bitter enemies and leaders of opposing militias foreswore violence and co-founded a youth organization that mediates conflict and builds peace. Tanenbaum helps them and their fellow Peacemakers in Action enhance their skills. These aren't the Dalai Lamas and Desmond Tutus of world; they are relatively unknown peacemakers who are changing the world.

MAKE A DIFFERENCE TODAY

Sometimes, looking at the big picture can be overwhelming because there is so much hatred and suffering in the world. Instead, focus on one doable piece at a time. Like a financial investment, your investment in change will grow over time and may even surprise you by the value it accrues. Take that first step today.

HER LIFE IS AN OPEN BOOK FOR GIVING
Patricia Schroeder, President and CEO, Association of American Publishers

Publishers.org

After serving twenty-four years as the popular Representative from Colorado's First Congressional District, Patricia Schroeder became President and CEO of the Association of American Publishers (AAP) in 1997, determined to make a difference. While in Congress, she was Dean of Congressional Women and co-Chair of the Congressional Caucus on Women's Issues for ten years. Schroeder made history as the first woman to serve on the House Armed Services Committee. Among causes she fiercely championed were work and family, children's issues, free speech, education, and protection of intellectual property. A member of the National Women's Hall of Fame and the Colorado Women's Hall of Fame, she also is an author and dedicated activist for change.

> *You can't wring your hands and roll up your sleeves at the same time. So choose!*

—PATRICIA SCHROEDER

My mother was a teacher who always worked in low-income areas because they were the most challenging. She would come home with incredible stories about jailed parents, fights, and deprivation. We'd hear how these little ones struggled every day with things that would be impossible for most adults to deal with. Her stories made me realize that we were totally blessed, and that not everyone had a family life like ours.

My mother's influence continued to help me make decisions. In college I joined the civil rights movement and advocacy for the mentally ill. After graduating from law school I worked as a *pro bono* attorney for Planned Parenthood and Denver Fair Housing and got involved with literacy, where I discovered that reading is an on-ramp to everything else in life.

Community service was always a hallmark of my congressional office. One weekend I came in and saw that there were dozens of roses in the office of one of my staff members. She told me an incredible story of how she had quietly worked behind the scenes to help a man whose daughter and mother had been caught in Dubrovnik, which was then being shelled by the Serbians. Inspired by his need and without asking anyone's permission, she had found an Italian ship captain who promised to transport his daughter and mother out of Dubrovnik. The man had been refused help—even laughed at—by the State Department, but this woman, who had one of those incredible helping minds, solved it. He never forgot her—hence the roses—and neither did I. Those were the kinds of inspirational people I had around me.

Today, I'm reaching out, especially on behalf of children, through AAP. Millions of American children start school without ever having seen a book, and they are almost doomed to do poorly. The number of kids who don't have any written materials at home is just appalling. We're living in an environment where everyone is bombarded with video and other technology, but you still have to be able to read. Third-grade boys and other non-readers aren't going to make the effort unless they have something they really want to read. At the association we're trying to make books accessible any way we can through several exciting literacy projects.

As we're living longer these days, I see our lives divided into thirds. First you learn, then you earn, then, but not only then, you should return. There's a new chapter out there for many people—an opportunity to give back so much more than they could in earlier, busier years.

Make a Difference Today

Think about it. If someone looked in your checkbook tomorrow, what kind of a profile would it show? Would people see that designer shoes were your priority, or would they see that you'd written checks to organizations that are making a difference for others? Beyond the money, it's a matter of how much you're willing to give of yourself, and understandably that's different at different times in your life. Look close by—you can make a difference right in your own back yard, so roll up your shirt sleeves and stop wringing your hands.

CHAPTER 3

Leading the Way with Nonprofit Giving

L eaders around the world teach us that caring for another human being is the essence of our human rights. They show us through their own generosity that caring is the right thing to do. These role models choose to leverage their circle of influence by structuring expectations for others to make a commitment to a worthwhile cause. They have a variety of names, positions, titles, and faces, but they all share a belief in caring for others and a mission to spread that belief to everyone they know. They have found enormous benefit in promoting giving, and they lead the way not just with their minds but their hearts.

As you read about how they learned the lessons that shaped their belief in giving, think about your own experiences. Have you had role models in your own life who have shed light on the importance of giving? Have you strived to follow their example? Each of us has met at least one person who embodies the spirit of giving. Who comes to mind for you? How can you begin today to more closely and purposefully emulate that person?

You'll note that the people you meet in this chapter came to their missions of giving to others through many different avenues. Though all are agents of social change and all inspire others to work for change, their approaches are unique. There's no single right or wrong path to enlightened giving. We all must simply keep our eyes open for opportunities and seize them.

Author and speaker Stedman Graham notes that, "Mentoring is another way to be a leader. Mentoring is an art, and throughout the years you learn how to do it. When we mentor and share our knowledge, we give validation to another person and giving our time says you must be important. True giving is done without an ego involved, and you give without expecting anything in return. Our calling is to help other people, which manifests into something powerful. That's why people who mentor are leaders, because they realize they can help others by organizing the resources and helping another person invest in themselves, in education, and knowledge about life. Mentoring is giving power to others."

As you read about amazing leaders who are working and mentoring others to help change the world around them, this is in itself an opportunity to be inspired. They offer innovative approaches to giving, and they rely on their personal skills, interests, and backgrounds to make their contributions. Leading takes commitment as well as courage. When you choose to lead, you take on responsibility for the actions of others. Never easy. But few things in life offer as great a sense of fulfillment as creating change through a personal vision to which you attract others.

DIVIDED WE FAIL

Jennie Chin Hansen, President, AARP; Robin Talbert, President, AARP Foundation; with Ellie Hollander, Chief People Officer, AARP

AARP.org

The story of Dr. Ethel Percy Andrus, AARP's Founder, has been told many times—for good reason. It is the story of a visionary woman whose life was defined by the idea that <u>it is only in the giving of oneself to others that we truly live</u>. It is the story of a passionate advocate who believed she could make the world a better place by doing the right thing. And, it is the story of how one person's exemplary life became the template for a culture of giving that has flourished at AARP since day one.

Someone somewhere once said that when you contribute to a conversation, that simple act of sharing a view or speaking up permanently changes the conversation. This is a very powerful notion: that what we say—or, in the case of taking action, what we do—can change the world around us. We can inspire, motivate, encourage, and we can make someone's day, just by choosing to give or to act.

This way of thinking continues to thrive at AARP, as the organization marks its fiftieth anniversary. Since 1958, AARP has been the nation's leading nonprofit membership association for people aged fifty-plus. With its community service pedigree,

AARP uses the collective voice and collective action of its forty million members to enhance the quality of life for all generations. It succeeds because giving is what animates everyone—volunteers, staff, and leaders—at AARP. It is and always will be the lifeblood of this great organization.

This makes for a unique workplace. Ellie Hollander, AARP's Executive Vice President and Chief People Officer, notes that "AARP is a wonderful place to work and volunteer because its mission inspires each of us to give our personal best every day and to exercise our individual power to make it better for others. Not only for the members we serve but for the impact we can have on improving the quality of life for all as we age. This includes internal programs such as our employee crisis fund or our leave donation program, which enable us to give to fellow colleagues who may themselves be struggling with their own personal crises. Also, our community builders program gives our staff paid time off to volunteer in their local communities. As Dr. Andrus said, "It is only through the giving of oneself to others that we truly live."

And it all began, of course, with Dr. Andrus, educator and social innovator. When she retired after years of teaching, she grew concerned about the plight of retired teachers, many of whom simply could not make ends meet. Dr. Andrus discovered that a favorite former Spanish teacher was living in a chicken coop because she had lost her retirement savings on a bad land deal, and the chicken coop was all she could afford on her $40-a-month pension. Dr. Andrus was dumbstruck. She launched a campaign to secure health insurance for retired teachers, making the case to company after company that profits could be made by insuring older Americans.

Her dedication paid off. Dr. Andrus established a successful pilot program for New York's retired teachers, and soon thousands of retired people wanted to know how they could get health insurance. Dr. Andrus used this experience to launch the National Retired Teachers Association, and then, in 1958, at the age of seventy-three, she formed AARP, now the largest, most successful public interest organization in the country.

Dr. Ethel Percy Andrus changed the conversation on health insurance for retirees, and she did so by challenging the deprivation she saw, refusing to take no for an answer, and pioneering a way forward. Years later, as AARP came into its own under her leadership, Dr. Andrus coined a signature line that would perfectly capture the AARP ethos: "What we do, we do for all."

Today, this ethos remains the principal frame for all AARP activities as well as the beating heart of AARP's voluntarism, advocacy, and philanthropy. With its sights trained squarely on the immense task of ensuring that all people have access to affordable health care and lifelong economic security, AARP is able to draw on deep, time-honored traditions of giving and mobilize an extraordinary array of resources to that end. The organization, for example, is fortunate to have over forty-six thousand volunteers reaching out on its behalf annually to more than three million people. That is a lot of giving power.

And while this culture of giving does indeed permeate every corner and every level of AARP, it is the organization's affiliated charity, the AARP Foundation, that is charged with the responsibility of stewarding and showcasing this prized asset. The foundation's President, Robin Talbert, is keenly aware of the importance of upholding the legacy of AARP's founder and doing everything possible to encourage giving as a lifestyle.

Talbert observes that, "Through small acts of kindness and large social initiatives, AARP is making a difference. When Dr. Ethel Percy Andrus discovered a woman living in a chicken coop, she got mad. And she got busy organizing, which led to a lifetime dedicated to change and social justice. We're carrying out Ethel's dream today, not just for older people but for everyone, by helping the most vulnerable attain financial security and health care. To me, AARP stands for the best in civic engagement, promoting individual dignity with volunteerism at our core. We provide scholarships, job training, consumer information, and access to benefits—a lifeline for those in need."

That it is. The AARP Foundation runs the largest free, volunteer-run tax preparation and assistance service in the country. The Foundation's Money Management and Benefits Outreach programs help older or disabled people manage their finances and access critical information. Foundation resources enable seniors to make their lives better by assisting with the high cost of prescriptions, providing training opportunities for securing employment, and serving as an ally in the fight against fraud. And the Foundation's

Women's Leadership Circle is offering new ways for women to approach mid-life by helping them to enhance their financial security through skill training and education.

Talbert knows a bit about creating opportunities and why we must all establish our own personal relationship with giving. "Life is truly a blessing. My mother was a teacher in the South when schools there were finally desegregated. She worked to make our high school welcoming to the new African American students. She was a strong woman who was a role model for caring and equality, so it was a natural progression for me to go into public interest work. I've spent my career working to provide opportunities for those in need. Today, when a Tax Aide client thanks us for the $200 refund that will be used for a new pair of glasses, I understand the need, and am so heartened that the AARP Foundation is here to help."

In retrospect, the story of Dr. Ethel Percy Andrus has not only fashioned a grassroots giving sensibility *within* AARP. It has, as well, attracted leaders *atop* the organization who are innately drawn to this ethos, to this way of being. AARP's current President, Jennie Chin Hansen—like Dr. Andrus, an educator—sees herself as a steward of knowledge, and, in turn, sees her stewardship of AARP's culture as a form of giving.

Hansen, the first boomer and the first Asian American to head the organization, now plays a significant role in advancing, perhaps, the most important initiative AARP has ever engaged in, designated Divided We Fail (DWF). *AARP launched Divided We*

Fail to raise the voices of millions of Americans who believe that health care and life-time financial security are the most pressing domestic issues facing our nation. Hansen observes that, Divided We Fail" is about identifying what we have in common rather than focusing on differences. Unified, we are reaching out to lawmakers and policymakers to advocate for change. Regardless of who occupies the White House or is elected to Congress, our initiative is about helping people secure affordable health care and lifelong economic security. These are people issues, not partisan issues."

It is this kind of visionary thinking—that things can always be made better by giving, by participating, and by doing what is right for those in need—that has echoed for more than fifty years at AARP. It will forever be a part of the organization's identity.

Jennie Chin Hansen is President of AARP. A consultant and RN who teaches nursing at San Francisco State University, she served for twenty-five years as Executive Director of On Lok, Inc., a nonprofit family of organizations providing primary and long-term care community based services in San Francisco.

Robin Talbert is President of the AARP Foundation. A lawyer and activist, she has held leadership positions across the Foundation and AARP for nearly twenty years.

Ellie Hollander is Executive Vice President and Chief People Officer for AARP, where she is charged with maximizing the engagement and performance of AARP's nearly 2,500 paid staff and providing resources and ongoing learning support for its impressive cadre of volunteer leaders.

MAKE A DIFFERENCE TODAY

Volunteering with seniors can be one of the most satisfying ways to deliver direct service. Nursing homes love visitors, especially those accompanied by children and pets. Older adults living at home often need a hand with yard-related tasks or simple inside repairs. In exchange for an hour of your time you can expect perspective, wisdom, and friendship. To identify opportunities, check with your local AARP chapter, social service agency, or faith-based volunteer organizations. Remember, together we make a difference, and we can succeed.

GIVING THROUGH EMPOWERMENT
Marc Morial, CEO, National Urban League

Nul.org

Founded in 1910, the National Urban League is an historic civil rights organization whose purpose is to empower African Americans to enter the economic and social mainstream. The oldest and largest community-based movement of its type, the Urban League played a key role in the twentieth century civil rights movement. The organization originally counseled black migrants from the South, helped train black social workers, and worked to provide educational and employment opportunities. Later in the twentieth century, the explosion of the civil rights movement led the Urban League into new directions as it became a visible leader in the movement. These included fundraising and planning the historic 1963 March on Washington. In later years, training and leadership opportunities, youth outreach, and voter education became priorities. In 2003, former New Orleans Mayor Marc H. Morial was appointed the League's eighth President and CEO. During his years in city hall, Morial helped significantly beat back crime, reform the city's police department, establish youth programs and ignite a flailing economy. City leaders called on the former mayor for leadership and courage when the city was ravaged by Hurricane Katrina. At the Urban League, Morial created the first Legislative Policy Conference and secured a $200 million equity fund for urban based businesses through the new markets tax credit program. His strategic direction and leadership have helped promote economic empowerment, health, civic engagement, and racial justice.

> *A community is democratic only when the humblest and weakest person can enjoy the highest civil, economic, and social rights that the biggest and most powerful possess.*
>
> —A. PHILIP RANDOLPH

I believe in civic tithing, proportional giving in accordance with one's ability. I think that people should commit to give back to the community in time, talent, and treasure. Many people give back within the context of their professions, for example teachers, people in government service, and those involved in civil justice. But I believe there's a way for *everyone* to give back—it can be as simple as tutoring or mentoring a colleague at work. My father was a civil rights lawyer, and my mother was a teacher and social activist. They were involved in everything—the church, politics, civil rights, and neighborhood issues. So I grew up believing that's what everybody did. I remember as a little boy of about nine being out on the campaign trail with my father during his run for Sate Representative of New Orleans. There was this wonderful sense of freedom and fun as I was allowed to run around at church picnics and voting rights events. At the time I had no idea these experiences were consciously influencing decisions about my life's work, but they were.

After law school I joined a law firm, but I soon realized the work was not going to be fulfilling for me even though it paid well. So I started my own law business, and about 25 percent of the work I did was *pro bono*. This allowed me to decide on the causes and cases that interested me. If I wanted to represent a South African exile seeking asylum, I didn't have to check with anyone first! If I wanted to challenge the constitutionality of a law on behalf of someone who couldn't pay me to do it, I could make that choice. It was an opportunity to balance success with significance, and it's something I believe everyone can do in their own way.

Good works are contagious, and small examples of giving and reaching out really make a difference. I encourage and challenge people to recognize that to those to whom much is given, much is expected, required, and demanded. I really believe that when we try to complicate giving by asking too many "whys"—we lose the point. To me, the point is simple, clear, and unambiguous: One day you or someone you love might be the one who needs a helping hand, a hand up, or maybe even a hand out. It's not just people who amass things who leave a legacy. People who reach out and touch others leave a legacy, too.

Today's Urban League is focused on a five-point strategy. We're empowering youth, economic growth, health and quality-of-life, civic leadership, and civil rights. We do this by reaching out in many different ways—from providing college scholarships to focusing on early education, home ownership, entrepreneurship, community service, and removing barriers to racial justice. But we don't do these things alone. The Urban League has a staff of about three thousand, but our programs thrive because of the involvement of some thirty-five thousand volunteers across the country who give tremendously of their time and resources.

Make a Difference Today

Model the behaviors you most admire and serve as a coach or mentor to someone with similar interests who could benefit. Think of how your time, talents, or treasures can make a difference. Volunteer in your community, and get involved in a nonprofit leadership position. Giving of any kind is a habit, a learned behavior, so become a role model and be the example for others to follow.

ORDINARY PEOPLE DOING EXTRAORDINARY THINGS
Rob Parker, CEO, Kiwanis International

The name "Kiwanis" comes from an American Indian expression meaning "we share our talents." Everyone's heard of Kiwanis, but how much do most of us know about Kiwanians extraordinary efforts to serve? Rob Parker is CEO of Kiwanis International, a volunteer organization with a single, extraordinary purpose: to change the world, one child and one community at a time. The members—260,000 adults 320,000 young people—also share their love and compassion with exceptional results. Their good works range from child abuse prevention to safer playgrounds and making hospital visits less traumatic for young children. At ninety-one years old, Kiwanis is coming of age, says Parker. In fact, he's leading a re-invention of the organization to focus on the next generation of servant leaders.

Nothing is so contagious as example; we never do any great good or evil which does not produce its like.

—FRANCOIS DE LA ROUCHEFOUCAULD

A servant leader is one who is focused on someone other than him or herself and whose purpose in leading is to make the world a better place. But servant leaders are not necessarily the charismatic, out-in-front types. They're the workhorses, not the show horses.

They're the humble people who give credit to others when things go well, and when things go wrong they look in the mirror for solutions. At Kiwanis, we believe in the powerful combination of personal leadership and character development—it's giving that starts in the head and heart, but it's also about acting with the hands and feet.

In Kuala Lumpur, Malaysia, an inspired Kiwanian was concerned about the status of children with Down syndrome. He inspired others with his vision that things could be, and should be, better. As a result of his passion, there are now seven centers in Malaysia serving those who had basically been cast aside, forgotten by society. Now these very special young people are being taught useful work, and their communities are learning acceptance. I visited one of these centers, and I'll never forget the hugs I got from those wonderful children who were so proud of what they were learning and contributing.

In the name of ordinary people doing extraordinary things, our members are sheltering the homeless and raising money for pediatric medical research. They've bought and delivered tens of thousands of trauma dolls that help children in pediatric hospitals understand what's happening to their own bodies. But what sets us apart from other service groups is our focus on leadership. If somebody teaches you to lead, they've improved your life forever. If they teach you to become a leader, they've helped you extend your circle of influence so that you can improve the lives of others.

When we announced our goal of reaching a million volunteers by 2015, our one hundredth anniversary, business as usual stopped. Big, outrageous dreams forced us to feel deeply, think strategically, and lead passionately. Suddenly we could see over the horizon. The impact of a million hearts and two million hands will be felt by children across the globe. Can you imagine the difference we can make? I can.

MAKE A DIFFERENCE TODAY

The earlier we learn in life that it's not all about us, the earlier we can pass from significance to success. What is the distinctive set of talents that describes you? Can you find a way to combine those talents with time *and* money? That puts you in the giving zone, where anything is possible.

To Whom Much Is Given Much Is Required

Bonnie McElveen-Hunter, Chairman, American Red Cross

RedCross.org

As the first woman to Chair the American Red Cross and one of the country's leading philanthropists, Bonnie McElveen-Hunter, Founder and CEO of Pace Communications, knows a great deal about the workings of the giving heart. Each year, victims of some seventy thousand disasters turn to the Red Cross for food, clothing, shelter, and solace. The mission of the Red Cross—to prevent and relieve suffering in the United States and around the world—has changed little since it was founded by Clara Barton in 1881. Although the Red Cross is not a government agency, it was chartered by Congress in 1905 to "carry on a system of national and international relief in time of peace and apply the same in mitigating the sufferings caused by pestilence, famine, fire, floods, and other great national calamities."

Each year, more than a half million volunteers help deliver Red Cross hope and relief to the needy, to military members and families, and to the victims of hurricane, cyclone, flood, and fire. The Red Cross was on the scene when disaster struck the Gulf during Hurricane Katrina, during the devastating 2008 earthquake in China, when floods washed away lives and property in the

Midwest, and when families were burned out of their homes during western wildfires. Through the Red Cross, another four million volunteers annually give blood, the gift of life.

Bonnie McElveen-Hunter is a dedicated philanthropist whose involvement includes membership on the International Board of Directors of Habitat for Humanity and chairmanship of the Alexis de Tocqueville Society of the United Way. She is Founder of the United Way Billion Dollar National Women's Leadership Initiative, which has raised $500 million to date. Her business and civic credentials are equally impressive. For more than thirty-five years, Pace Communications has produced magazines for companies including Four Seasons Hotels and Resorts, Toyota, Delta, United and US Airways, among others. Pace Communications is ranked as one of the top 175 women-owned businesses in America by *Working Woman* magazine. As former U.S. Ambassador to the Republic of Finland, McElveen-Hunter spearheaded two highly successful initiatives: *Stop Child Trafficking: End Modern-Day Slavery*, and the *Women Business Leaders Summit® for Finland, the Baltic, and Russia.* Another summit was held in Jordan for the Middle East including women from Iraq, Palestine, Syria, Bahrain, Lebanon, Egypt, etc.

Mighty causes are calling us—the freeing of women, the training of children, the putting down of poverty— all these and more…may we find a way to meet the task.

—W.E.B. DuBois

Our collective destiny stands in need of 100 percent of our resources, male and especially female! My belief in the power of giving comes from my faith—a belief in the widow's might that everybody has an opportunity to give.

I saw first hand the results of Red Cross efforts to assist the people of Ethiopia, where three-quarters of the population does not have access to clean water and four out of five live without proper sanitation. Ethiopia suffers from one of the highest rates of child malnutrition in the world and has the sixth largest number of people living with HIV/AIDS. Red Cross efforts to provide clean water through a partnership with the Ethiopian Red Cross Society were incredible to witness. When I saw the life-changing impact of a simple hand pump in one project-served village in the Zeway Zone, I wrote in my diary: "Before the hand pump the women of the village had to walk more than two kilometers to find water ... not only is the lake far, the water is full of microorganisms and unfit for drinking. Without clean water, who can have a safe and healthy life?!" The arrival of the pump meant clean, healthful water right in their village—no more several-mile walks to find water and more time to attend school or earn an income. The people of the community changed their habits and became accustomed to using the pump. In another nearby village, the American Red Cross and Ethiopian Red Cross built a water cistern to support students at a local school. This meant the kids could stay in school all day instead of searching for and collecting water or leaving class early to get water from home. Where others see problems, we look for solutions. That defines the giving spirit of the American Red Cross.

I believe business is the most powerful force in the world; it ushers in social, political, and economic change. Unlike any other sector, business has the ability to raise and improve lives across the world. My concern has always been, how do we create successful business models that will continue to improve lives, especially the lives of women and children on whose shoulders poverty weighs so heavily?

MAKE A DIFFERENCE TODAY

In the end, all we ever have is what we give away. We come into the world with nothing, and we leave with nothing. Invest in the potential of others. If you don't have money to give, consider becoming a blood donor or make phone calls for your local Red Cross chapter. When disaster strikes, don't wait for someone else to call to volunteer. Reach out. You can save a life.

KNOWLEDGE IS POWER
Dr. Marion Morra, Chair, National Board of Directors, American Cancer Society

Cancer.org

The American Cancer Society is the largest nationwide nonprofit, community-based volunteer health organization dedicated to eliminating cancer as a major health problem. It does this by preventing cancer, saving lives, and diminishing suffering through research, education, advocacy, and service. Since 1975, Dr. Marion Morra has been an avid volunteer for the society, a member of its national board of directors since 1997, and current Chair. An internationally recognized expert in cancer control, outreach, and communications, Dr. Morra is President of Morra Communications, a medical and health communications consulting firm. Previously, she was Associate Director of the Yale Comprehensive Cancer Center.

Established in 1913, the Society has thirteen chartered divisions throughout the United States, more than three million volunteers, and a local presence in more than five thousand communities nationwide. In the last half century, the society's research program has supported numerous groundbreaking discoveries. Second only to the federal government in research funding, the society awards more than $100 million annually—mostly to promising new investigators whose work offers lifesaving future results. To date, forty-two society-funded investigators have won the Nobel Prize.

Dr. Morra's life has been devoted to educating the world about cancer, and she is co-author of four best-selling self-help books including the path-breaking *CHOICES: A Sourcebook for Cancer Information*. Millions of copies of her pamphlets have been distributed free to patients and their families, and they continue to be primary sources of information today.

The greatest wealth is health.

—Virgil

The good news is that we've made an amazing amount of progress battling cancer. When I first started in 1975, most people died from the disease, and today there are ten million cancer survivors! We're providing hope, new options, and have learned how to prevent cancer and treat it. We hope in years to come to solve the cancer problem, and things are progressing at a very fast pace. Cancers are being detected earlier and earlier, and they are more curable.

Knowledge is so important. Cancer patients often say, "Getting cancer treatment is like going to a foreign country where you don't speak the language." So they don't even know what to ask. Knowing the right questions helps you get the right information.

When you add the time and brainpower you give as a volunteer to other people's time and brainpower, it's possible to make a tremendous difference. Each person's journey with cancer is different. No one is immune from cancer, but it's our personal responsibility, to make a difference. Cancer touches one person and one family at a time, and the result is many unmet needs. You can help in so many ways—from simply listening to someone who has a cancer diagnosis about their concerns and their needs, pitching in to help with duties related to the home and children, offering rides to the hospital or doctors' appointments, and so much more. Regardless of your age, you can be a volunteer.

Volunteering should be fun, so choose something you enjoy. When I was installed as Chair, my niece noticed how many people were hugging each other and asked, "Aunt Marion, how many hugs have you gotten today?" It's a great way to be involved.

I've made a large number of friends as a volunteer, and I can say with certainty that the American Cancer Society has the most incredible volunteers I've ever met. Expand your world and do something good for someone else and at the same, you will do good for yourself.

As Dr. John R. Seffrin, national Chief Executive Officer, says, "Giving—whether it is of time, talent, or finances—is a simple way for all of us to bring joy into other's lives as well as to our own. At the American Cancer Society, we see firsthand every day the power that one individual can have against the face of something as terrible as cancer. Our organization is proof that a little time truly can do a great amount of good."

MAKE A DIFFERENCE TODAY

Don't wait for someone to tell you how to live a healthy life. Take charge, get informed, and live a healthy lifestyle that helps prevent cancer. You should eat five fruits and vegetables a day, stop smoking, exercise, get adequate screening—colonoscopy, mammography, and cervical pap tests, and take charge of your own health.

In Praise of School Board Member Volunteers

Anne L. Bryant, Executive Director, National School Boards Association

NSBA.org

Although everyone knows that teachers change the world, the incredible influence of school board members also makes an enormous difference. The country's 95,000 local board members make up one of the nation's most committed groups of volunteers. Anne L. Bryant is Executive Director of the National School Boards Association, which represents board members in towns and cities across the country. Its mission is to promote excellence and equity in public education through board leadership. School boards are the ultimate expression of grassroots democracy. Members voluntarily advocate for children, working within their communities to help students reach their potential. NSBA-affiliated members represent nearly 15,000 school districts and more than 47 million public school students. Anne Bryant has a deep commitment to education. She was Chairman of the Simmons College board of trustees and is Vice Chair of the Universal Service Administrative Company, which provides discounted telecommunications service to schools, libraries, and low-income individuals. Before joining NSBA, Bryant served as CEO of the American Association of University Women.

Do something for somebody every day for which you do not get paid.

—ALBERT SCHWEITZER

Education has always mattered a great deal in my life. For years, my father was treasurer of the Perkins School for the Blind in Boston, famous for students including Helen Keller and her teacher, Annie Sullivan. I grew to share my father's love for this very special school—a connection that continues to this day. I also became very close to my *alma mater*, Simmons College, a school where I and so many young women studied in hopes of becoming great leaders in the professions. During the late 1960s, I protested the absence of a student on the board at Simmons, and to my surprise, I was asked to join the board soon after graduation. I served for thirty-five years, including as Chairman, and Simmons remains very close to my heart.

When we think about education, we think about reading and math, which of course are so important. But when you ask parents why they care so much about the schools their kids attend, they'll often talk about learning character, being culturally aware, and becoming enriched citizens who can hold a good job and give back to the world around them. We all want these things for our children, and often the decisions about whether they will have them rest with our school boards.

Board members come from every walk of life. They are Republicans, Democrats, and Independents, men and women, young and old. They are of every race and come from every type of professional background—from farmers to lawyers and Indian chiefs. They represent much more than their communities … they represent our kids. These are the people who have to find a way to put resources into the arts even when there's nothing left in the budget. These are the people who go out and personally raise money to send a great high school band to a national competition. They're the ones who make the really tough decisions about closing a failing school. To me, they reflect the best kind of citizen governance, different from other kinds of elected officials. That's because once they're elected, school board members move beyond what they did or didn't vote for and support local superintendents, teachers, and labor groups, all in the best interest of the students.

About 90 percent of all children in this country attend public school, and 90 percent of 55 million is a lot of children. Volunteer board members have a tough job. Their views are often strongly opposed, and they have to be tough-skinned to fight for what they believe in. A board member who votes to change a school boundary may suddenly discover enemies she had no idea existed. A board member who argues against hiring new teachers will hear about it every time he walks into the supermarket or the hardware store! This is tough work, but so very important.

MAKE A DIFFERENCE TODAY

One of the most challenging and rewarding ways to serve your community is by serving on its school board. If you've been looking for a way to contribute, and if you have a passion and a vision for education, make your interest known. The school board movement needs volunteers who care deeply about improving teaching and learning.

Or, get involved in education. Tutor or coach, get engaged any way you can.

CHALLENGING YOUR COMFORT ZONE
Martha Mertz, Founder, ATHENA International

athenafoundation.org

Martha Mertz is an accomplished businesswoman and the Founder of the ATHENA Award Program and served as President of ATHENA International from its inception in 1982 through May, 1999. The ATHENA Leadership Model focuses on the collaborative leadership style often exemplified in women leaders while also recognizing the importance of traits such as courageous acts and fierce advocacy in the pursuit of excellence. The model includes Authentic Self, Celebration and Joy, Collaboration, Courageous Acts, Fierce Advocacy, Giving Back, Learning and Relationships. It is presented to a woman—or man—who is honored for professional excellence, community service, and for actively assisting women in their attainment of professional excellence and leadership skills.

What is honored in a country will be cultivated there.

—PLATO

To understand the ATHENA Award, you have to look at women during the times when they were functioning as leaders but were invisible. No one identified women as leaders. They were considered helpers. Places couldn't run without women, but giving-back-to-the-community time was unpaid and always has been. In creating the ATHENA Award, I believed we could raise up one outstanding female leader at a time and ultimately change the face of leadership. In fact, our award is based on a new kind of leadership. It's frequently not the most visible individuals who are honored. Originally we established three criteria, and they've remained the same: The recipients have achieved the highest level of excellence in their profession; they must be individuals who have given back of their time and talent to their community; and they must have opened leadership opportunities for others, particularly women.

In 1982, the first recipient was Dr. Marylee Davis, and at the time she was working at Michigan State University as a liaison between that large institution and the community. She brought a new sense of collaboration, attention, and resources to circumstances within the community where I lived, and she improved life for everyone. She showed the type of leadership that has a strong component of giving back.

We started the award in our community to raise awareness of the leadership role that women play. It was a public, visibly important event in the community, and it has spread since then to more than 350 communities in this country, Canada, Russia, China, India, and England. Our mission is to encircle the globe honoring women as leaders. This award isn't about winning or losing. It's a way to say, "Thank you for inspiring us."

Inspired giving means passionate devotion to a cause. It means unwavering advocacy and often times rising above oneself or one's comfort level. It takes courage to envision the possibilities and then to inspire and motivate others to accomplish something. Passionate devotion to something gives us the wings to leap off a cliff and fly.

I've done a lot of traveling for speaking engagements, and in each city I meet the strongest, most selfless, most exceptional women and men. These people are finding purpose and meaning by giving back—through their compassion and outreach within their community. Their names range from ones you wouldn't know to stellar names you would, but it's an amazing force bringing a new kind of emphasis not based on how important "I" am. Their leadership is pulled from nurturing. This type of leadership coming from women isn't exclusive to women, but it's our responsibility to teach this type of leadership to everyone. Our world is in a dysfunctional time. It's time to influence, in small ways and large, the guidance for our future.

We each have some combination of gifts that can leave a legacy in this world, and that's what giving back is all about. Years ago my husband, Edward Ingraham, found a quote from Plato that sums up our mission: "What is honored in a country will be cultivated there." You have to have a vision to see the world in a different way and see the profoundly different possibilities. Once that vision lodges itself in your soul, it will never let you go. A small good idea is like a burning ember. If you give it enough time and enough space and bring energy to it, it has the power to grow into a force that can change the world.

Make a Difference Today

Giving back requires us to be leaders, to inspire others to make a difference while we are trying to make a difference ourselves.

Taking on this responsibility also requires us to move beyond our comfort zones, even take risks. Such a risk can be overwhelming, but when we take it, through our belief in the need for giving, we enlarge ourselves and subsequently make for a better world.

CHAPTER 4

Corporate Giving

This chapter is one of the most significant as we honor and pay tribute to a sampling of major corporations who have identified meaningful programs and ways to give back to their communities or to their world communities. Business leaders at their best are givers, and those who do generally have higher performing employees and gain better performance and thus, stock value.

Those who are champions of corporate social responsibility are our heroes on so many fronts. They keenly recognize the importance of encouraging employees to give of time and dollars. We salute the synergy that comes from motivating their workforces and giving back. We salute other workers and labor unions and those who give of their time and money where it counts. Here, learn of the innovation, passion, and examples of giving expressed in these business profiles. Add your own business story of work for community or environment. And know that today's young people use corporate giving as a barometer for selecting their job and career.

Some of these major corporations are global players, and others are working with their local communities where there is a need. Many are matching employee contributions at a minimum of dollar for dollar. Others are giving time off to participate in a cause of your choice. Whether the environment or mentoring in inner-city schools, the millions of hours of time and the millions of dollars show forces of giving back. The opportunities for you and your companies are vast, and innovative volunteering and philanthropic contributions do make a difference. You can do more today and make for a better tomorrow. These stories will give you a mission-driven pride in business giving.

BETTER WORK, BETTER LIFE
Tig Gilliam, CEO and Joyce Russell, President, Adecco North America

Adecco.com

Adecco is a Fortune Global 500 company and the global leader in recruitment and workforce solutions. The Adecco Group delivers an unparalleled range of flexible staffing and career resources to clients and associates. Its vision is "better work, better life." As the world's largest employment services group, a business that positively impacts millions of people every year, Adecco provides a human connection to jobs, community, and giving back. Tig Gilliam is the CEO of Adecco North America and provided the story of humanity in human resources.

> *The purpose in giving back in our profession means "better work and a better life."*

> —ADECCO VALUE

As the world leader in human resource solutions for millions of people, Adecco's vision has gone far beyond the reach of simply "better work, better life." Adecco touches millions of people around the world every day.

Better work, better life represents our company's spirit. If you walk the halls of any of our 1,200 branches across the country you will see, hear, and feel the spirit of Adecco Group. Everyone who works on our team comes to work everyday to help people find new and better opportunities for themselves so they can improve their careers and their personal lives as well.

Better work, better life isn't something we've taught or trained people to do. The tagline was developed as a reflection of who our 6,000-plus colleagues are and what they bring to the people we serve everyday.

We provide 500,000 people in the United States with jobs and paychecks annually. Providing a sense of purpose in giving back is helping fuel Adecco's growth. Helping people find jobs is noble and a unique challenge which inspires us each day.

What organization do you want to be a part of? Most people want to be part of something that really does make a difference and doesn't just make claims in the annual report. Social responsibility is part of the fabric of our culture at Adecco. Because our jobs are to help people find career opportunities, naturally the type of people we attract to our organization have it in their nature to reach out and help others.

We believe there is shared value in what companies like Adecco do: what we do is good for us only as long it is also good for individuals, our clients, the economy, and society at large. A sound economy and society create a better environment for us to operate in, with talented people seeking better work and a better life and companies seeking to grow. We see good business and strong contributions to our society as interdependent.

Our daily work provides benefits to our employees, our clients, shareholders, and suppliers, with governments, society at large, and, of course, with the environment. Building fair and lasting stakeholder relationships is how we enhance trust and reputation, strengthen our competitive position, achieve long-term growth, and thus contribute to a better workplace for all.

Part of my motivation for changing careers was to be part of a company that makes an impact on people's lives, a company where people feel a part of the organization; that's the feeling you get at Adecco. At our national leadership meeting in Orlando, our colleagues organized a team building exercise to bring people together and ensure camaraderie. Clusters of Adecco company leaders came together and helped build bicycles and then raced them. At the end of the company races, we donated the bicycles to local kids. This is just one example of our culture of better work, better life—something that makes all of us proud to be part of Adecco.

Adecco helps people at all points in the socioeconomic spectrum. Whether it's their first job, the bridge between jobs, or a second career, Adecco places people with the right employers.

Many of our innovative programs make me proud:

- *The Athlete's Career Program* helps Olympic athletes after their Olympic careers.

- *The Renaissance Program* assists the older generation in finding second career and part-time jobs. We are proud to work with the AARP in this partnership.

- *Career Connections* is designed to work with the United States military personnel and their spouses upon relocation to find work. Their new community needs and requirements can make it difficult to adjust to their new environment, but Adecco prides itself on making a smooth transition. Adecco helps find resources for all programs to ensure the best candidates are matched.

- *Jobs for America's Graduates* helps at-risk youth, can get them through high school, and land their first job.

When Hurricane Katrina hit, Adecco employees wanted to take off work so they could help with relief efforts. This is the culture that Adecco has adopted since its inception. Joyce Russell, Adecco USA President, shares the story of the disaster response. Adecco colleagues got moving, literally, to help in the aftermath. Mobile recruiting teams visited evacuees in shelters across the Southern states. This face-to-face approach, giving practical support, helped get over five hundred evacuees back into work and able to start rebuilding their lives. This makes us grateful to be in a position where we could help and proud to be part of an organization that takes action when we have friends, family, colleagues, and neighbors in need.

Adecco is also a champion of corporate social responsibility and diversity practices.

We take action to encourage the inclusion into the workforce and society of disadvantaged people, such as the disabled. Lois Cooper, who leads our Office of Diversity and Inclusion at Adecco, shares our belief that diversity is not just about doing a good thing, but about a better way to do things. Diversity collects better points of view, and with that comes diverse backgrounds and experiences. Bringing that different perspective to each and every business decision is a good thing, and it increases that expectation with our clients. And there is a sincere sensitivity to the disadvantaged, and all of this makes a contribution to business and to life.

MAKE A DIFFERENCE TODAY

Have you ever asked someone what you can do to help, and then listened to the answer? *Stopped and really listened* before taking action? Being a person others can count on with the knowledge that you'll come through is a true blessing in life. How good it feels to be that someone!

FEEDING THE HUNGER FOR GIVING
Michel Landel, CEO, Sodexo Group

Sodexo.com

Sodexo, a leading integrated food and facilities management services company, serves 50 million customers daily in eighty countries across the globe. But this world-class company strives not just to feed the body—Sodexo is also committed to feeding the soul. Founder Pierre Bellon set the vision decades ago when he said, "Our mission is to improve the quality of daily life for people wherever and whenever they come together." In 1996, Sodexo launched an initiative to fight hunger and its root causes. It takes a big company with a big heart to launch a plan with the ambitious name 'STOP Hunger,' but that's just what Sodexo has done by creating an inclusive, effective program that engages employees in this ongoing battle.

Michel Landel joined Sodexo in 1984 as Chief Operating Manager for Eastern and North Africa. He became CEO of the North America business in 1999. Although Sodexo has always had a generous heart, its commitment to activism and philanthropy took off in 1996 when Landel and others participated in a Boston-area hunger walk. Involvement grew into STOP Hunger, and in 1997 Sodexo Servathon, an annual month of service, was introduced. Each April, thousands of Sodexo employees volunteer their time and raise money to help hunger-related charities.

The war against hunger is truly mankind's war of liberation.

—JOHN F. KENNEDY

The world is facing a food crisis—rising demand, soaring oil prices, and climate changes are contributing to an epidemic of hunger that is putting basic nutrition out of reach for the 800 million people considered malnourished across the globe. And these numbers are only expected to increase as society struggles to address the immediate needs of those less fortunate while simultaneously seeking long-term solutions.

The nature of Sodexo's business is to serve others; in fact, our employees touch the lives of millions of people everyday in communities around the world. But what sets us apart is the distinct culture of giving that has evolved within our organization. The desire to give back in both large and small ways is deeply embedded in the fabric of our company and is carried out by employees at all levels.

Take, for example, a Rhode Island District Manager who wondered what students at risk of hunger did when they did not have school lunch to sustain them. Out of his concern arose Sodexo's Backpack Food Program that provides food to children and families at risk of hunger on the weekends. Every Friday, select students leave school carrying nondescript backpacks filled with nutritious, easy-to-prepare food provided by local food banks and packed by Sodexo volunteers.

Sodexo's business, the culture of employee giving, and our emphasis on corporate values is at the core of a deep and long-standing commitment to being a driving and creative force that contributes to a world that is free of hunger and malnutrition. Leveraging the passion of our people and the unique infrastructure of our organization, Sodexo launched our STOP Hunger initiative under my direction in 1996. This initiative focuses on fighting hunger and its root causes by engaging Sodexo's global workforce in the ongoing battle.

A major part of our business is providing foodservice, and the word serve is a vital part of that. We have a social role to play in providing nutritious meals to students, patients, corporate employees, and other customers. An essential aspect of our mission is to participate in the social and economic development of the communities in which we do business.

For example, in Madagascar Sodexo partnered with the United Nations Food and Agricultural Organization (FAO) to conduct a survey in the Fort Dauphin region to determine local production capacity and identify development opportunities to maximize, over time, local sourcing possibilities. Through the Malagasy non-government organization Tsaratraka, Sodexo is supporting agricultural development through the production of local vegetable farms. Dozens of community farmers are learning farming techniques that increase supply and help to compensate for the lack of a regional market.

Quite simply, for any global company, being a good corporate citizen is first and foremost just the right thing to do. Second, it makes good business sense. Sodexo's mission extends beyond our operations and into the communities where our employees and customers live and work.

Our commitment to community involvement is readily apparent in the stories of Sodexo's Heroes of Everyday Life—employees from North America who are honored every year for outstanding contributions related to the fight against hunger. The stories are poignant—simple acts making big differences.

For example, in Allentown, Pennsylvania, E. Scott Daniels organizes large-scale holiday dinners and heads a celebrity chef event that raised $450,000 for Meals on Wheels. For the past thirty years, Alice Sutton of Burlington, Vermont, has collected more than 40,000 pounds of food for a Vermont food bank. Since 2000, Dan Durand of Eagan, Minnesota, has engaged other Sodexo employees to prepare and serve meals at a local community center, and to date has served more than 6,000 meals.

Sodexo's emphasis on serving others can be seen in our mission to "improve the quality of daily life for people wherever and whenever they come together." This mission revolves around three core values: service spirit, team spirit, and spirit of progress. Commitment to these values is seen in the actions of every employee and in every area of our business sphere. We do not drive results at the expense of our values, and we hold our people accountable for living them.

Sodexo's contributions to food banks and hunger organizations are praiseworthy, but our commitment to addressing the root causes of hunger goes far beyond that. Our real goal is empowerment.

We want to give people hope, not just a meal; a future, not just a momentary solution. Sodexo's hunger related programs include job training and partnerships with organizations that provide opportunities for people to better themselves and their families. We also actively recruit and hire individuals that have participated in these programs.

Our culture encourages employees to identify a need and then work to come up with a solution. In Chile, Sodexo partnered with our client, Rigoberto Fontt Technical School, in Colina City to launch a unique hotel and catering training program. This program targets young people in disadvantaged areas where job opportunities are limited. Similarly, in the Ancash region of Peru, Sodexo partnered with our mining client, Minera Antamina, to develop training programs for people from the underserved Andean communities. In just six years, 622 people have been trained to take positions in the hospitality industry.

We want to provide more than a job—we want to provide an opportunity for a career, regardless of education or experience or background. We want our people to have a very strong sense of what they can bring to others.

MAKE A DIFFERENCE TODAY

Each and every human has the power to shape the future of our world. We do this through our personal and professional actions. Do what you can to contribute to a future where people are respected for who they are, and where differences are leveraged to create innovations that continually improve the quality of life for everyone.

A SNAPSHOT OF ENGAGED LEADERSHIP
Essie Calhoun, Vice President and Chief Diversity Officer, The Eastman Kodak Company

Kodak.com

Essie Calhoun began her career as a sales representative for the company in 1982 and was elected Vice President in 2000. As Chief Diversity Officer, Calhoun works to strengthen inclusion initiatives among employees, customers, and suppliers. Her duties include oversight of Kodak's corporate philanthropy and community involvement worldwide. Essie Calhoun is a born leader who has created a number of organizations to identify and nurture leaders. Among these are United Way of Rochester's African American Leadership Development Program and the Kodak Youth Leadership Academy. Her good works have been widely acknowledged with honors, including the Martin Luther King Commission Individual Award and the NAACP Outstanding Leader Award.

> *If you have much, give of your wealth. If you have little, give of your heart.*
>
> —ARAB PROVERB

I believe that we *are* our brothers' keepers, and that goes not only for individuals but for corporate citizens as well. Like people, companies must acknowledge that giving back is the price they pay for existence on this earth. When businesses touch communities, we also touch our employees, who make our companies what they are. Ultimately for me and for Kodak, it is about knowing that something has changed for the better as a result of our actions and contributions. My own mother died three weeks after I was born and my father passed less than three years later. I watched my maternal grandmother give tirelessly of herself to raise me, but only as I matured did I really appreciate this level of selflessness.

I've learned that the best leaders are also servants, engaged in problem solving and willing to roll up their sleeves rather than criticize. At Eastman Kodak Company, that culture was established by our Founder, George Eastman. In the early 1900s, he made several contributions to Tuskegee Institute and contributed to the building of Hubbard Hospital at Meharry Medical College. Mr. Eastman named the first woman to the Kodak board of directors. He was also the Founder of the Community Chest, which later became the United Way. Today, volunteerism is part of the DNA here at Kodak. It is a huge component of our corporate culture. Our Chairman and CEO, Antonio Perez, sets the tone through his own personal philanthropy and engagement. When I moved from sales into public affairs, I never knew that this is where I would discover my life's work through connecting with communities at the grass roots to identify and help meet needs, working with at-risk kids, providing the basics of food and clothing, or through grants and product donations that improve people's daily lives.

Make a Difference Today

If you want to serve the underserved, get out of your comfort zone. Assess your knowledge base, skills, and talents, and commit to making the time to share them. If you're new to volunteerism, consider a local hospital or nursing home. These are great places to start, and they always need assistance. If you're a little bit further along and know your passion, consider starting your own nonprofit! In this diverse and interdependent world, making the world a better place for others makes it a better place for you, too.

INSPIRED GIVING
Marilyn Carlson Nelson, Chairman, Carlson Industries

Carlson.com

Marilyn Carlson Nelson is Chairman of Carlson. Born in 1938 as the Gold Bond Stamp Company, today Carlson is a global leader in the marketing, travel, and hospitality industries and ranked among the largest privately held corporations in the United States. Marilyn Carlson Nelson, named one of the world's one hundred most powerful women by *Forbes* magazine, has recently completed a decade as CEO of Carlson, leading this global company with a social consciousness and a compassionate heart.

You make a living by what you get. You make a life by what you give.

—WINSTON CHURCHILL

To me, inspired giving occurs when the giver actively dreams beyond their own time and place and acts on a desire to transcend self and somehow touch the life of others. I have had many excellent "giving mentors" in my life: chief among them was my father, who inspired me and who helped build a community that even today believes in a strong quality of life and ensured business vitality. Through the years, the Twin Cities has proven to be a community that cares down to its very (and sometimes, aged) bones.

Years ago, when I was involved in a fund-raising drive and engaged in door-to-door solicitations, I visited a neighborhood house (an old school with several agencies housed in it). There I observed an older African American woman slowly setting the table for lunch. No one knew where she lived or even how she got there every day; kept close to her was a bag carrying all her worldly possessions. The old woman told me her name was Laura and that she would be ninety in one year.

Noting her advanced age I said, "Laura, I understand you've been setting the table for lunch all these years; couldn't perhaps someone else do this for you now?" At this, Laura became very upset, and told me she wouldn't think of giving up the job. "Oh no, I do it to give back!" she said.

This exchange reminded me that one needn't *have* a lot to be able to *give* a lot. In fact, one of the most wonderful things I've learned along the way is that, as a percentage of their income, those with the least often give the most, and as Laura made so clear, their gifts are not limited to money. However, make no mistake, there are times when financial support is critical.

I am most proud of Carlson's work as a co-Founder, with Her Majesty Queen Silvia of Sweden, of the World Childhood Foundation. The foundation works with street children, who are particularly vulnerable to illness, abuse, and human trafficking. Certainly, Carlson's large financial gift has been important to the success of Childhood. But just as important have been the other ways we've been able to help. For example, in March, 2003, at UNICEF headquarters in New York, we became the first, and to date only, large U.S. travel signatory to the ECPAT Code (End Child Prostitution and

Trafficking). The code commits organizations to fighting trafficking of children, especially for sexual purposes. Carlson's signing of the code made international news and, in the United States, brought a hitherto undiscussed problem out of the shadows. At the time, it helped the effort even more than money might have.

Thereafter, we trained our people to recognize and report signs of trafficking, and soon grassroots employee efforts were popping up, resulting in additional financial support and, just as important, the deep personal support of individual human beings in the fight on behalf of the world's children. Speaking to the hearts of Carlson colleagues all over the world was, indeed, a great gift to the future of childhood.

Suppliers and partners also took our lead. Some gave money. Others, like our Radisson partner in Cancun, took action and helped introduced the ECPAT Code to Mexico; our partners at the Japan Travel Bureau—that country's largest travel agency—did the same in that country. Our early and vocal leadership within our own circle of influence has proven to be an even greater gift, one that continues to give today.

Again and again throughout my life and career, I have seen that good people often need only be given an opportunity to step up and do the right thing—and they usually will and do. Sometimes they just need the gift of inspiration. Such has been the case with Carlson and our support of World Childhood.

Whatever the gift—whether large or small, of money or of time—I believe the giving spirit is enhanced when a personal connection is made with those to whom you are giving. I suggest you find a way to meet the recipients of your caring. I have done that with the street children of the world; I have done that with the ninety-years-young Lauras of the world. When you look them in the eye, learn their names, and find out what makes them tick, your giving will be truly inspired and will benefit the both of you more than you can ever know.

MAKE A DIFFERENCE TODAY

The giving spirit is enhanced when you have a connection with those to whom you are giving. Find a way to meet the recipients of your caring. Look them compassionately in the eye, ask their names, and find out what makes them tick. Your giving will be inspired when you connect with a cause greater than yourself.

A Small Gift Opens Doors
Maribel Aber, Vice President, NASDAQ OMX

NASDAQ.com

As a globally recognized brand, NASDAQ OMX, the world's largest exchange company with trading, technology, and public company service capabilities that reach across six continents, provides a platform for philanthropic organizations—helping to raise awareness of important work of various charitable foundations. NASDAQ OMX understands giving back to the community. Through the televised NASDAQ Opening and Closing Bell Ceremony, NASDAQ OMX has helped to highlight nonprofit organizations by offering the opportunity to ring the bell in celebration of their achievements and success in a given sector. The corporation has also provided visibility to nonprofit organizations by showcasing public service announcements on the MarketSite Tower, the largest stationary LED screen in the United States. As well, NASDAQ OMX has hosted large organizations including the American Cancer Society, Habitat for Humanity, Fresh Air Fund, and Muscular Dystrophy Association, as well as smaller groups like Project Sunshine, Manhattan Youth, and MOUSE.

With exchanges in North America and Europe, NASDAQ OMX serves as a trading venue for multiple asset classes and supports the development and operations of more than sixty exchanges in more than fifty countries around the world. Through offices in over twenty countries, NASDAQ OMX delivers services and forward-thinking technology to drive capital formation, transform business, and fuel economic growth around the world. Vice President Maribel Aber of NASDAQ OMX is responsible for establishing the strategic direction, operations, and technology for the NASDAQ MarketSite, home of the NASDAQ Opening and Closing Bell Ceremony and MarketSite Tower.

Wealth is the ability to fully experience life.

—HENRY DAVID THOREAU

I am proud to be associated with NASDAQ OMX, an organization that, in addition to hosting its listed companies, has readily offered the nonprofit community a platform to drive visibility for their causes. It is particularly meaningful to have had the opportunity to help to empower today's youth. Every young person who visits NASDAQ OMX could potentially be the next entrepreneur to build an innovative business and someday ring the bell as a listed company. Many successful NASDAQ CEOs started their businesses at a very young age.

Having hosted more than 150 NASDAQ Opening and Closing Bell Ceremonies for nonprofit organizations, I have met some of the most influential people who lead the charge on behalf of charitable organizations. I feel humbled by the time and energy that volunteers devote to their organizations' missions. Recently, I have been inspired by the work of the Rainforest Foundation Fund, founded by Sting and Trudie Styler and chaired by Franca Sciuto. I have been touched by their efforts to protect the world's rainforests and have signed on to volunteer my time and support for the fund.

True success is measured by how much one gives back. I have met so many interesting people who have come to ring the bell, from politicians to athletes and from celebrities to CEOs. But many of the most successful people have been the ones that come and speak from their heart about what they are most passionate about, whether it is focusing on the environment, education, or finding the cure to a debilitating disease. Their dedication and commitment are genuine and inspire people to give back. We are all activists. We are all responsible for our world. How much we choose to give back is what, I believe, defines us and makes our lives more meaningful.

I am driven to help make a difference, big or small, in the life of one person. I have so much, and it takes so little to give back. The biggest victories can come from even the smallest acts of giving. Whether you plant a tree, tutor a child, or donate blood, the results of your time and effort are tremendous. A small gift opens doors, provides hope, and an opportunity for making the world a better place. And, when you embrace the idea of giving back and integrate it into your life, the rewards are priceless.

MAKE A DIFFERENCE TODAY

Every business can reach out to charities and nonprofits and give them visibility and support. Be creative in your approach, and let it reflect the purpose and image of your organization. Engage your corporate public affairs and communications departments as well as a foundation if your company has one. Corporations are like individuals—they feel better when they are reaching out.

WHERE BEST FRIENDS ARE MADE
Maxine Clark, Founder, Chairman, and Chief Executive Bear, Build-A-Bear Workshop

BuildABear.com

The teddy bear is the quintessential image of childhood. Build-A-Bear Workshop, Inc. brings the warmth and comfort of teddy bears to life. It was created in 1997 by Maxine Clark, the former President of Payless ShoeSource, Inc. and a former Executive of the May Department Stores Company. Build-A-Bear does business in a spirit of friendship and trust by providing an interactive retail entertainment experience. The stores are teddy-bear themed with original fixtures, murals and artwork. Employees, better known as Master Bear Builder Associates, assist guests and share the experience at each stage of the bear-building process. The stores are places where memories are created and new favorite bears, bunnies, dogs, and kittens are born and loved.

An important part of the company's philosophy is giving back to the community through the Build-A-Bear Workshop Bear Hugs Foundation. Among giving programs is Champion Fur Kids which raises funds to help fight pediatric cancer, diabetes, and autism. The company also partners with the World Wildlife Fund. A dollar from the sale of each special WWF plush animal goes to protect endangered animals and habitats. Since the beginning of the partnership in 2000, Build-A-Bear Workshop has donated over $1 million to the fund. The company also supports children's literacy and other causes of the heart.

Childhood is the most beautiful of all life's seasons.

—ANONYMOUS

One of the things I'm most proud of is that we've been able to contribute more than $10 million to good and important causes. After 9/11 our stores were flooded with people creating bears for needy children. And since then we've been asked to help in the wake of so many natural disasters. When we respond, we always try to share the joy of giving by getting children to participate. Every one of our bears has a heart, and part of the process of making a bear is making a wish that's "inserted" with the actual heart. We love hearing children wish good things for others.

A number of years ago, Gail Geopolo's precious daughter Nikki died from a rare bone cancer. Nikki was a sweet and generous child who often made bears for other sick children on her way to her chemotherapy treatments. Before she died, we were honored to be able to grant Nikki's wish by creating a bear to support children's cancer research. The Champ Bear, as it's known, is purple, Nikki's favorite color, and all the proceeds go to fighting this disease. Of course we can't make a bear for all the deserving children and causes out there, but Champ Bear is a symbol of our commitment to listen and to care.

For us, it's not about being in the Fortune 500 or the Fortune 100. It's about caring more and being more connected. It's about giving in a fun and creative way. Sometimes the stories are touching, and sometimes we cry, but that's OK. We're not afraid of being human. After all, we're in the business of bringing teddy bears to life.

MAKE A DIFFERENCE TODAY

Involve children at an early age with the joy and benefit of giving. Find age-appropriate ways to spread kindness and help kids see that they can make a difference. Start a tradition by choosing an annual service project that involves the whole family once a month making or delivering food, coaching sports at a Boys & Girls Club, or volunteering at an animal shelter. Kids are natural givers; nurture this gift to create a lifetime of givers.

IF YOU WANT TO MAKE A DIFFERENCE
Esther Silver-Parker, Senior Vice President of Diversity Relations, Wal-Mart Stores

WalMart.com

Esther Silver-Parker grew up in a giving family and has pursued a career that reflects deep concern for the world around her. Since 2006 she has been Senior Vice President of diversity relations for Wal-Mart. She is responsible for planning and execution of the company's efforts in community relations, philanthropy, and retention. Silver-Parker led AT&T's Public Relations and Corporate Social Responsibility Programs and was President of the AT&T Foundation. Early in her career she worked in pubic relations and as a journalist for *Essence* magazine and the *Review of Political Economy*. On behalf of the Board of Global Ministries she has traveled to and written about health and living conditions for women and children in the Congo, Burundi, and Kenya. Silver-Parker has been recognized widely for her achievements by the Congressional Black Caucus, the Harlem YMCA, and the National AIDS Fund, among others.

If you want to lift yourself up, lift up someone else.

—DR. MARTIN LUTHER KING, JR.

We grew up poor in rural Eastern North Carolina. My grandmother had a huge garden, and the vegetables she grew were given to people who couldn't afford food for their families. My six brothers and sisters and I were expected to work in the garden every day after school. Other kids would tease us when they saw us gardening, and I'd ask my grandmother why we were being picked on in this way. She'd tell me it wasn't about the teasing, it was about the fact that people were hungry, and it was our duty to share what little we had with them. Like my grandmother, my parents were very clear about our responsibility to give back in some way, not just financially. They helped us understand that if all you could do was pick up trash on the streets or tutor someone in school that was enough. They wanted us to think larger, to embrace other people and causes.

Since I first started working, I've always contributed a portion of my bonus to a scholarship fund I set up in my parents' names at Dillard High School in my hometown of Goldsboro, North Carolina. I take great joy in presenting it every year to a deserving student to honor my parents who never had the resources to go to college.

At Wal-Mart it's a matter of corporate citizenship. We have a responsibility to the communities from which we generate resources and in which our associates live and work. We've given grants to train Hispanic nurses to help people in local communities navigate the health care system. We help displaced women get back into the work force and provide scholarships that send Native Americans to college.

Make a Difference Today

A lifetime of focus on oneself yields limited returns. There are needs in every neighborhood and every community. Nonprofits are a wonderful way to get connected; you can also learn a great deal that will help you professionally. Many people perfect skills as volunteers that help them make important progress in their careers. You're also likely to gain a valuable network of friends and acquaintances with whom you share something valuable—a desire to serve more than yourself.

WHEN YOU GIVE BACK, IT COMES BACK
Mary Wong, President, Office Depot Foundation

OfficeDepotFoundation.org

As President of the Office Depot Foundation, Mary Wong is a champion of giving. Office Depot had always been a caring company, but its focus on corporate philanthropy gained new purpose after September 11, 2001. In fact, philanthropy is so key to Office Depot's mission that the foundation is a separate nonprofit entity, giving it the opportunity to raise additional funds in support of its mission beyond what the company can invest. The foundation is committed to helping 50,000 students graduate from high school rather than become middle-school dropouts. It is also committed to helping nonprofits become more entrepreneurial, strengthening local communities, and providing assistance for disaster relief and recovery.

> *You get the best out of others when you give the best of yourself.*
>
> —HARVEY S. FIRESTONE

In 2001, I was in Chicago with an Office Depot Senior Executive who was in town to deliver a speech. We were walking in Cabrini-Green, the housing project synonymous with urban blight and poverty. Ahead of us was a young girl who was walking shoeless, carrying her school supplies in a paper bag. "Mary," my colleague asked me, "What can we do about this? I'm here to give a talk about how young people can be whatever they want to be, but how can that happen when some of them don't even have shoes?" That moment continues to inspire the work of the Office Depot Foundation.

We've learned and done so much since then. Our National Backpack Program puts colorful new backpacks containing essential school supplies in the hands of amazing, deserving kids. Imagine this: if the nearly 1.5 million backpacks we've donated since 2001 were stacked on top of each other, they would be as tall as 148 Empire State Buildings! Yes, we're a large corporation, but we believe in grassroots giving. At every store grand opening, we choose three local nonprofits and hand each a $500 check. In 2007, we helped more than 2,200 charities. We were the first company to pledge $1 million to the Red Cross as Hurricane Katrina was approaching the Gulf Coast. We also try to help solve problems, so when a series of wildfires struck Southern California, we provided funds for economic assessment studies and planning to help residents and businesses get back on their feet.

Although I don't believe in fate, I do believe that things happen for a reason. I was diagnosed with epilepsy at age fourteen, and I saw firsthand what the kindness of people can mean. I've found that by giving back it comes back … many times over. I'm not a rich person, but I'm a lucky person. When my young nephew was about ten, he presented me with a gift. He had visited the Holocaust Museum in Washington, D.C., and he chose a poster for me. It was a collection of words—*kindness, purpose, respect, honor.* "Aunt Mary," he said, "this reminds me of you."

MAKE A DIFFERENCE TODAY

Ask yourself the hard questions: What do you stand for? Why do you give? What do you want to give? Figure out what you want your giving to mean, and then make something happen. You have to take this step first so that you can take the next steps that help others. Take some time to draft a personal mission statement. What's important to you as a giver? Put it in writing and try to make sure the work you do is aligned with the statement.

A LEGACY OF LIFTING OTHERS
Pat Harris, Chief Diversity Officer, McDonald's Corporation

McDonalds.com

McDonald's is the leading global foodservice retailer, serving nearly 56 million people in 118 countries every day and providing support for each of the communities in which it operates. Pat Harris, Vice President and global Chief Diversity Officer, is "still lovin' it" after more than thirty years with the company.

From the very beginning, Ray Kroc, McDonald's Founder, insisted that its "three-legged stool" of franchisees, suppliers, and company employees give back to the communities that supported them, according to Harris. This grassroots effort created the first Ronald McDonald House—a haven for families with seriously ill children—in 1974, and today there are 271 Ronald Houses in thirty countries around the world. McDonald's created Ronald McDonald House Charities (RMHC) in 1984, a foundation committed to children and families everywhere with a global network of local Chapters in fifty-one countries. RMHC has become one of the leading not-for-profit organizations across the world.

Volunteers are not paid—not because they are worthless, but because they are priceless.

—UNKNOWN

Harris started work as a secretary at McDonald's more than thirty years ago and was given the opportunity to advance to her current officer level. The corporate commitment to giving back fits perfectly with Harris' personal values. As she says, "People say you should give until it hurts, but I have learned that if you give a little bit more than that, then it doesn't hurt at all." Harris has passed the lasting legacy of this commitment to giving to her son and granddaughter as well.

Harris has received numerous awards and recognition for her contributions to the community, such as McDonald's Shining Light Award, the Chicago Metropolitan's YMCA Black & Hispanic Achievers Award, the King Legacy Award from the Boys & Girls Club of Chicago, Today's Expo for Black Women's Phenomenal Woman award, the Top 10 Diversity Champions in the Country by *Working Mother* magazine, and the Eagle Award from the International Franchise Association. Harris serves on the DePaul University Board of Directors' Institute for Business and Professional Ethics Committee, the Women's Leadership Board at Harvard University Kennedy School of Government, and is the chair of Breast Cancer Network of Strength (formerly known as Y-ME National Breast Cancer Organization).

McDonald's supports a great number of other charities as well, according to Harris. "Our belief in giving back to the communities we serve empowers people to seek out the philanthropic interests that appeal to them as individuals," she says. The example set by company leaders like Jim Skinner, CEO; Don Thompson, President of McDonald's USA; and Ralph Alvarez, COO extends throughout the organization right down to the people working in McDonald's restaurants. "When we see our top management living the vision of giving back in spite of their busy schedules, we are all inspired to do the same in every community around the world," Harris says.

"McDonald's believes that one person can make a difference, and I hope I will be remembered for trying to make a difference in the lives of people who needed help. In our jobs and in our communities, we are all in the business of lifting others up."

MAKE A DIFFERENCE TODAY

Think about ways you could give to a nonprofit organization by filing or even answering the telephone. Whether you are a pro on the computer and can volunteer your skills organizing an online database or by designing or improving an organization's website, your skills will be a welcome contribution. People power, putting our talents to work for others, is one of the best ways to give.

COOKING UP A CAUSE
Doris Christopher, CEO, The Pampered Chef

PamperedChef.com

Doris Christopher's belief in the importance of families gathering around the dinner table was the inspiration behind The Pampered Chef. The company she launched from her basement grew into a $500 million enterprise before becoming a part of the Berkshire Hathaway company. The Pampered Chef offers professional-quality kitchen tools directly to consumers through in-home cooking demonstrations. Today, more than 60,000 Pampered Chef consultants are at work in the United States, Canada, United Kingdom, and Germany.

When Christopher created Round-Up from the Heart in 1991, she turned The Pampered Chef into a company that cares about the world as well as its consultants and customers. Round-Up has raised more than $13 million by inviting customers to "round up" their orders to the next dollar to benefit America's Second Harvest (now Feeding America), The Nation's Food Bank Network. In 2000, The Pampered Chef joined the American Cancer Society to launch Help Whip Cancer®. Proceeds from specially marketed pink products benefit education and early detection efforts, and consultants and customers have raised more than $6.5 million to Help Whip Cancer®. Christopher has extended her philanthropic reach even further as Chairperson of the Direct Selling Association and its Educational Foundation. She is a member of the DSA Hall of Fame and has been central in DSA's efforts to link direct selling with worldwide social responsibility.

If you can't feed a hundred people, then just feed one.

—MOTHER TERESA

Once Pampered Chef began to catch on, we were overwhelmed with gratitude for all the people who had helped us and for the free enterprise system that allowed this success. It made us start to take a more formal look at our outreach and to carve out some resources to give back. The goal was to engage lots of people in this opportunity to get involved in something much bigger than any one of us. Over the years thousands of consultants and customers have participated—they're all part of an incredible gift.

We delight in serving meals and making life easier for families. So what could be more fitting than partnering with an organization that makes sure there is a place for *everyone* at the table, especially the less fortunate? I remember walking up the podium at The Pampered Chef convention in 1991 to announce our relationship with Feeding America. I was so sure that this was the right cause at the right moment, but I was also a little apprehensive because I was making a commitment for thousands of other people. As I began to speak you could hear a pin drop. There was a sense that everyone in the room was with me on this.

The difference we're making is so real. One afternoon as I was preparing to leave the office I got a phone call from a food bank director in Allentown, Pennsylvania. She had just been handed a check by a consultant (the checks are delivered twice a year, but now this is done directly to the food banks) and she felt she just had to call. "When the check arrived, it was like an angel from heaven," the director told me. "I had just heard from a large donor who had a truckload of potatoes available, but I didn't have a way to get them from the farm to the food bank. I called back immediately and told him to point that truck in our direction!"

MAKE A DIFFERENCE TODAY

There's power in pennies. It's a matter of finding a place to start, then building steadily toward a dream. Set ambitious goals for yourself as a giver and a doer. Big thinking and working steadily toward the goal pay off.

A LEADER WITH ALL THE RIGHT TOOLS
Julia Klein, Chairman, C.H. Briggs Co.

CHBriggs.com

Julia Klein owns C.H. Briggs Company, one of the largest independently owned building materials distributors in the industry. Her many honors include being named among *Women's Enterprise USA* magazine's top one hundred women-owned businesses, Pennsylvania's Best 50 Women in Business, and being a finalist in Ernst and Young's Entrepreneur of the Year competition. Through Klein's leadership, C.H. Briggs was twice named a national winner in the *Inc.* magazine/ Cisco systems Growing with Technology awards for its leadership in network technology and electronic commerce. Briggs has also received awards from *Kitchen & Bath Design News* for Innovative Supplier and Community Service. C.H. Briggs was also honored to receive the Frank R. Palmer Corporate Citizenship Award, the Employee Campaign Award, and the Eagle Award from the Berks County United Way. Klein received the 2004 ATHENA Award, a national program that promotes women's leadership and honors an individual for their business and community-service accomplishments.

> *For it is in giving that we receive.*
>
> —ST. FRANCIS OF ASSISI

Everybody is inspired for different reasons and toward different goals. I try to encourage individuals to find their own path, to inspire philanthropists who maybe don't have millions to give but want to do more than write a small check. The field of philanthropy has a lot of work to do to uncover people's passions and connect those individuals with smart organizations that are doing good work.

As a businesswoman, I think about philanthropy in the non-traditional sense of the word. For example, we employ 180 people, and so 180 families depend on us for their livelihood. On a basic level, when I see families who feel confident enough to buy a house, take a vacation, put their children through college, I feel fabulous about the investments we're making and the risks we're taking.

I had a co-worker who was suicidal, going through a difficult time. After trying to help him one evening, he ended up sleeping on our sofa because we were worried about leaving him alone. He got through the night and his dark period, but it remains with me.

The Caron Foundation, a famous drug and alcohol facility, gave me their community service award, and I was touched that someone remembered that story about caring in action. He made it through. To be in a place to make a difference in someone's life is what matters.

Caring is the rent we pay for living in the world. What else is the point? Everybody can be a philanthropist, and everybody can create change. You don't need to have millions of dollars to do it. When we do our United Way campaign in the office, we find that people who are making an hourly wage are the most generous because they are able to quickly identify with how easy it is to be in trouble. That always gives me great hope that everybody has the ability to be generous and a change agent.

The world is not a perfect place, and there's a lot of work to be done. No matter what interests you or worries you or inspires you, that's where you can start giving. Everyone can find their helping niche in the world—be it a village in Afghanistan, microfinance in a women's circle in Bangladesh, distressed urban kids in Reading, Pennsylvania, or orphans in El Salvador. When you find what moves you, you are called to action. You recognize the gaps between how you live and how other people live. That's very compelling. I believe in doing well by doing good and in giving back and paying it forward.

Make a Difference Today

People who postpone giving until they've amassed a fortune miss many opportunities to make a difference. Start small, and start today. Perhaps you'll see a jar on the counter to feed children or help stray animals. However, before you give, ask how your change will help that cause. Helping just one person in need can lead to bigger changes down the road.

CHAPTER 5

Giving in Action

Daily, we read or watch the news to learn of poverty, crime, suffering—one tragic story after the next. We do our best to be positive, to avoid surrendering to cynicism or despair, but sometimes the struggle can be difficult. In fact, it can be overwhelming. We complain about social ills and believe something must be done about them.

Some of us donate money to help remedy these ills. Millions give of ourselves, give of our time, in order to affect a real change. We can't be disheartened by the ferocity of need we see every day around us. One person can make a difference just as meaningful as can one organization.

These leaders demonstrate Giving in Action. They believe in solutions. They act and "do it now." They and the millions volunteering with them are agents of change. In this chapter you'll meet some amazing organizations and a number of people who are putting their concerns into action, who are giving of their time and their talents in large ways, who are making a difference as you can, too. Select your own Giving in Action plan.

CARING FOR THE CAUSE
Helene D. Gayle, MD, PhD, President and CEO, CARE

Care.org

CARE, one of the world's largest private humanitarian organizations, helps communities in the developing world tackle poverty. The staff of more than 12,000 across the globe work through an array of programs to address the root causes of poverty, with a focus on women. CARE has millions of supporters who care about the future of communities and the health and welfare of families.

CARE works in more than seventy countries around the world and aims to contribute significantly to the Millennium Development Goal of halving the proportion of people living on less than $1 a day by 2015. Helene D. Gayle, serves as CARE's President and CEO.

> *Every CARE package is a personal contribution to the world peace our nation seeks. It expresses America's concern and friendship in a language all peoples understand.*

> —PRESIDENT JOHN F. KENNEDY TO CARE

Dr. Helene Gayle of CARE shares that the scope of CARE's mission has changed considerably since its founding in 1945, when twenty-two American organizations came together to rush CARE packages to survivors of World War II. Thousands of Americans, including President Harry S. Truman, contributed to the effort. Over the subsequent twenty years, some 100 million CARE packages reached people who were recovering from war.

CARE, along with a few other organizations right after World War II, captured the hearts of the America public. We created the idea of the CARE package which today is a part of the American lexicon. Since that time, CARE has gone on to take that spirit of giving and extended it in seventy countries around the world.

Our sources of income are roughly $600 million a year with $130 million from the American public, including foundations, corporations, and individuals. When you think of the millions of people that are living on less than a dollar a day, you think what it takes to help them escape the trap of poverty, and $600 million is actually a small part of the solution.

We believe that if you can change a poor woman's world, you will change the life of her family and of her community. From the beginning, helping people in a tangible way and showing them how they could touch someone far away has been CARE's basic goal. We seek to help end poverty globally. One of the ways we make CARE relevant is helping poor women become empowered to obtain education and health care services.

CARE's focus is creating a solidarity movement between women in America and their counterparts overseas. Almost 75 percent of the poorest people in the world are women. If we can help them, we not only help their children but also strengthen their communities and societies. American women understand the struggle of raising a family, and we know that once they understand the poverty faced by women in other countries, they want to reach out and help.

MAKE A DIFFERENCE TODAY

CARE was one of the forerunners in the world of international philanthropy. Only 2 percent of all philanthropy in the United States goes to international aid and overseas development. Caring has a special meaning. Reflect on your capacity to care. When you support programs for women and children in your community and recognize the phenomenal needs around the globe, you can make a difference. Dollars go a long way when we invest in women and their families. Help your family and help others across the world, and know that your caring and financial support will have a significant impact.

NEW CLOTHES FOR A NEW LIFE
Joi Gordon, CEO, Dress for Success Worldwide

Dressforsuccess.org

Joi Gordon is Chief Executive Officer of Dress for Success Worldwide, an international grassroots organization that promotes the economic independence of disadvantaged women by providing professional attire, a network of support, and the career development tools to help women thrive in work and in life. Dress for Success has served more than 450,000 low-income women since 1997. In her role at the headquarters of Dress for Success, which oversees more than eighty-five affiliates across the globe, Joi is responsible for the continued growth and strength of the organization's infrastructure, programming, and global presence, securing resources for the worldwide office and affiliates and raising Dress for Success' international profile. In addition, Joi maintains close ties with Dress for Success locations around the world, providing them whatever support is needed.

> *Life's most persistent and urgent question is: what are you doing for others?*
>
> —MARTIN LUTHER KING JR.

Robert Half said, "Giving people a little bit more than they expect is a good way to get back more than you'd expect." I believe that the more you give, the more you receive in return. I get hundreds of emails a month from amazing women whom we have helped or whom I have met and mentored. There's one woman I recall who had been in jail and received a suit from Dress for Success when she got out. Now she's a General Manager for a restaurant chain! She wrote me an email after seeing a story written about me, saying, "I am so proud of you on the front cover [of a magazine.] You inspire me daily, and I see myself standing alongside a wonderful woman and an organization [that is] backing me and every goal I have ever wanted to accomplish." When you reach out and help people it makes them, in turn, want to give to others. Paying it forward is what happens at Dress for Success, where we give women something extremely important. They come in and receive suits, but they leave with something more much powerful. And receiving emails like this one is what motivates me.

It's so gratifying to hear from women all over the country about something I said or that Dress for Success has done. We become a friend to the women we help, and the support that we offer makes these women stand taller. I do what I do because of the pure joy of giving to others. My mother predicted my life would be centered on helping others, on sharing this joy. And she was right. A former attorney, I have always had a passion for helping women and young girls; it is one constant in my life and my true calling. I was raised by a single mother who saw in me her own vision of success. When asked on job interviews about her greatest accomplishment, she'd respond, "My daughter, Joi." She put me first in everything. I look at the women who walk into Dress for Success and often feel like I am looking at my mother. Most of the women are also single moms who want to provide better lives for their children.

So what does a new outfit mean? It means a new life. It means starting over and a fresh beginning. The suit is a symbol of success. Women put on a suit, look in the mirror, and in front of them is something—someone—whom they might never have seen before. In faux pearls and that treasured suit is someone successful looking back at them. And that is the first step to building self confidence. Their circumstances left them on an unleveled playing field, and what they want to do is to land jobs and become self-sufficient. The suits help them realize what is possible.

When we look in our full closets and say we have to clean them out or they're a mess or we have nothing to wear, someone else is looking in her closet and *really* has nothing to wear. I know I am very fortunate, with a closet full of suits, and that I have choices. But there are women out there who have nothing, and for them a suit becomes a life jacket. And by providing a woman with her life jacket you, too, can change a life. It really is that simple. People make giving far more difficult than it has to be. Going into your closet, pulling out a suit that you no longer wear, and sharing it with another woman can have a profound impact. Both women win. One has cleaned out her closet and feels fulfilled because she has helped a woman begin her journey towards success. The other now has her own power suit and can walk into her interview feeling confident and hopeful.

I look at my life and never question why I stopped practicing law. Being here has filled my soul, and I hope to continue to change lives be helping women dress for success on the inside and on the outside.

Make a Difference Today

Remember that a new outfit might simply mean new clothes to you, but to someone who is not fortunate enough to own even one suit it can become a new lease on life. Provide someone a fresh start today by donating a suit, an outfit, and help her recapture her hope. You can ensure that a woman embarks on her journey to a brighter future with a renewed sense of pride and purpose. All it takes is a suit.

VOLUNTEERS KEEP AMERICA IN BUSINESS
Ken Yancey, Executive Director, and Mark Dobosz, Foundation President, SCORE

SCORE.org

Small business is the engine that drives the U.S. economy. SCORE is a dynamic nonprofit association that pairs volunteer counselors (retired and current executives) with those launching new ventures. The skills and wisdom they share help make new businesses vibrant and profitable while offering volunteers the chance to give back. Since SCORE was founded in 1964, nearly 11,000 counselors have reached out to more than 8 million small businesses including Vermont Teddy Bear, Vera Bradley Designs, and Jelly Belly Candy. Headquartered in Washington, D.C., SCORE has 389 chapters across the United States and its territories. Ken Yancey is CEO of the SCORE Association, and Mark Dobasz is Executive Director of the SCORE Foundation.

The business of America is business.

—CALVIN COOLIDGE

There's a long tradition in this country of business volunteerism. A small town banker coaches Little League. Barbershops sponsor holiday food drives, and car dealers purchase uniforms for the high school band. SCORE keeps that tradition alive like no other organization and has advanced business volunteerism in exciting new ways.

There's a huge movement of social entrepreneurism and personal philanthropy in this country. In our fast-paced, disposable society, people love the feeling of being involved in what they contribute to. One impetus for that has been technology—it's easier for people to get engaged when they can understand what's out there, and the Internet makes that possible like never before. Once people see the options, they don't want to stay on the sidelines. One of the best things about SCORE is that those who benefit from the assistance are often inspired to become volunteers.

SCORE volunteers have helped create thousands and thousands of jobs and provide ways for businesspeople to develop and share wealth. So many businesses credit SCORE with their success, thanks to volunteer counselors like Les Fraser. Between 1973 and 2005, Les spent thousands of hours assisting hundreds of clients. A decorated World War II veteran and Founder of Casual Corner stores in Atlanta, Les got as much as he gave from his experience. His contributions were so significant that in 2007, SCORE created and presented him with the first Lester Fraser Entrepreneurship Award. It recognizes successful entrepreneurship and outstanding volunteerism, civic leadership, and vision.

The connection between SCORE clients and counselors like Les is tremendous. A great example is the three women who decided to open a bookstore. One day in a coffee shop they scribbled their idea down on a napkin and decided to go for it. They knew that if they didn't live their own dream, they'd end up working for someone else who did! SCORE counselor Hooper Wesley started by helping them develop a viable business plan. With his guidance, the FoxTale Book Shoppe in Woodstock, Georgia has become a flourishing small business with close ties to the community. The owners continue to meet with Hooper who loves to boast about their success.

Recently honored by SCORE for her service to the organization, co-author of this book and Les's daughter, Edie Fraser, shared these words with an audience of almost a thousand people: "We go the extra mile, often the one that makes the difference. We go hand in hand. We don't know the word 'can't,' as that is the word meaning defeat. We know the words 'can do.' Can is the word of vision and of service. As Abraham Lincoln said, 'I do the best I know how, the very best I can; and I mean to keep on doing it to the end. I can do it. I can give.' She continued with a poem:

> *It's you, with the "can do" who are dears*
> *We share a giving bond through the years.*
>
> *How enriched our lives have become*
> *Passion about giving no matter where we're from.*
>
> *We stand the test in a passion for giving.*
> *It's commitment to mission while living.*
>
> *Yes, we are each others best fan*
> *To guide us to service the best we can.*
>
> *We hold one another with a trust*
> *Giving while living is a must."*

Edie added, "The quality of a person's life is in direct proportion to their giving. We can find time to care. I follow the saying of Maya Angelou: 'If you find it in your heart to care for somebody else, you will have succeeded.' I spent five years with the Peace Corps staff, five years with the national poverty program after college, twenty-seven years on the board of Big Brothers, have served on numerous nonprofit boards, am now on the national board of SCORE, and have mentored more than two hundred interns and young people. Mission and service have immeasurably enriched my life."

John Ruskin said, "The highest reward for a person's toil is not what they get for it, but what they become by it." We get so much from giving. Eleanor Roosevelt said clearly, "The future belongs to those who believe in the beauty of their dreams." We are clear that dreams can be reality, that aspirations can become a strong mission. And Louisa May Alcott said, "Far away there in the sunshine are my highest aspirations. I may not reach them, but I can look up and see the beauty, believe in them, and try to follow where they may lead."

We have determination and a deep commitment. We must continue to try hard to follow the mixture of service with our busy lives. Giving can be contagious. Our will is a life of service. Giving is our legacy.

MAKE A DIFFERENCE TODAY

Support your passion, whether it's business or Scouts or coaching. There are so many great nonprofits out there, it's easy to find the right one. And remember that philanthropy is two sided. There's a personal side, which is giving yourself the opportunity to help someone else. Reach out while you're alive and can see the difference you're making.

Giving Light, Sharing Opportunity
Robert Goodwin, Past President and CEO,
Points of Light Foundation

PointsofLight.org

Robert Goodwin served as President and Chief Executive Officer of the Points of Light Foundation from 1995 until 2007. He joined the foundation in March, 1992, as Executive Vice President and Chief Operating Officer. Points of Light is a nonprofit organization whose mission is to grow the quantity and quality of volunteering in this country, and there are over 4,500 Points of Lights who have received this distinguished recognition. Together, with the Volunteer Center National Network, the foundation engages millions of people more effectively in volunteer service that helps to solve serious social problems in thousands of local communities throughout the nation. Robert Goodwin also created Connect America, a collaborative effort led by the Points of Light Foundation to engage every American in helping solve serious social and community problems through volunteering.

It is in the shelter of each other that the people live.

—Irish Proverb

It is imperative that there is a spirit or culture of giving because it is the only way available to the average person to bridge the divide. We call this social capital, which helps to strengthen the fabric of our democracy. In times past when someone had their house burned down or lost a loved one they could always depend on family, friends, and neighbors and in effect build a safety net that kept that individual from being isolated. Volunteering helps build social capital. John Dunne reminds us: "No man is an island." Giving becomes a means for extending ourselves on behalf of others who require some form of human support or the warm embrace of their neighbor.

When we give to others, we gain a sense of personal satisfaction and personal fulfillment that is more rewarding for the giver than the recipient. It enables us to feel that their lives count, and we are more than units of personal consumption. Contributing to the well-being of another is the greatest gift of all. Giving is an obligation for those that have benefited from a free and democratic society. The only way we can hope to extend or prolong the same benefits of this society is by taking personal responsibility.

My mother was the most inspirational and influential person in my life and vital to the end at 102. Her favorite quote was, "Service is the price we pay for our room and board on earth." The spiritual training was a part of my early life because, as I was taught, to whom much is given, much is required. Recognition is important because it is an affirmation that encourages people to replicate the example of those who are cited and recognized.

Our goal is to double the number of volunteers over the next five years and increase business and corporations to go into the community of volunteers and involve more people in lower income communities and providers of service. We aspire to a more caring and giving society where more people will accept their personal responsibility to improve the quality of life through selfless acts of service.

One of the most memorable stories that still haunts me to this day is the story told of the little boy who was shuffled from foster home to foster home. He looked into the eyes of the latest social worker interviewing him for his next placement and said, "I ain't nobody's nothing." That story has stuck with me because I know the impact a loving mentor or tutor or volunteer could have made in the life of that child, reassuring him of his value and helping to usher him into a life of productivity and self-fulfillment.

The Points of Light award program is one of many awards. Recognition is just a representation of a small plank in a larger platform that we have built to encourage more and better volunteers. I'm very proud of helping to build a culture of service in our country.

Make a Difference Today

Find out how you can make a difference at work, and remember that one person can inspire a community or workplace to come together as a team. If you know someone deserving of praise for his or her volunteerism, nominate that individual for an award or other recognition. Let the media know about their efforts or make a donation to the cause they care about. Be a ripple and a reflection of their kindness. Spread the word and emulate the deed.

The Power of a Wish
David Williams, President and CEO,
Make-A-Wish Foundation

Wish.org

Every forty minutes in the United States, a child's wish comes true thanks to the enormous efforts of the Make-A-Wish Foundation, the world's largest wish-granting organization. It started in 1980 with the wish of young Chris Greicius to become a police officer. Since that time, the now global organization has said yes to more than 161,000 children with life-threatening medical conditions. The magic is made a possible by a network of more than 25,000 volunteers who serve as wish granters, special events assistants and fund-raisers.

Although it is one of the most well-known charities in the world, Make-A-Wish retains its grassroots character. Its unchanging mission is to bring hope, strength, and joy to seriously ill children and to their families. Through its life-changing work, the foundation works to make sure that deserving children of tomorrow will have an opportunity to share the power of a wish like the thousands who have gone before them.

Sometimes we stare so long at a door that is closing that we see too late the one that is open.

—Alexander Graham Bell

I received a letter from the father of a wish child that was so heartfelt it made me cry. His daughter's wish, which was granted seventeen years ago, was to go to Disneyland with her family. The dad wanted to tell me how much the experience had affected the whole family. Reading on, I learned that the girl has now graduated from college and is planning to work in a hospital as a child health specialist. And the dad had become a counselor at a camp for children with cancer. So you see the impact of a wish is really wide and deep. I meet people who have been volunteering with us for years, and they routinely tell me that they get more out of the experience than they give.

Another phenomenon we're seeing much more of is kids who are giving away their own wishes. Whether it's swimming with the dolphins or going to Disneyworld, they're taking a step back and saying, how can I use what I've been given to help someone else? One amazing young lady wished to start her own orphanage in Zambia. At last count, she was well on her way, having raised nearly all of the $60,000 required! Another teen's wish was to throw an unforgettable party for kids living in a homeless shelter in her hometown of Phoenix. And one extraordinary young lady's wish was to raise enough money so that the wishes of every wish child in her home state would come true!

Most people are naturally drawn to fixing things—to making the world better. We all want to believe we made a difference on earth beyond just making money or enjoying ourselves. We're at our very best when we take a step back and think about who we are and what we're supposed to be doing. I think our most human moments are when we're giving to someone else—a wish, a hug, time, money, or just an ear for listening.

MAKE A DIFFERENCE TODAY

Find a personal connection with the mission of an organization you choose to support. There are so many wonderful nonprofits doing important work, but you'll have the most impact if you have a passion for what's going on. If a particular choice doesn't work out, know that another, better match is out there. Don't give up on giving; the world needs you.

At Work for a Great Cause
Tory Johnson, Founder and CEO, Women For Hire,
Women For Hire Foundation

WomenforHire.com

Since 1999 Women For Hire's core career-related services have successfully targeted college-educated, professional women, yet its founder, Tory Johnson, formed the Women For Hire Foundation in 2007 to specifically serve low-income, disadvantaged women by helping them to realize their career potential.

Most of these women are single mothers with the sole financial responsibility of raising their families. Many seek the foundation's counsel after long-term unemployment caused by eldercare responsibilities or other physical and emotional challenges. Johnson believes that access to training and a hand up could mean the difference between minimum wage versus a livable wage, inconsistent hours versus a steady schedule, and no benefits versus health insurance and paid time-off.

From traveling to areas of crisis—as Johnson did in the aftermath of Hurricane Katrina and her staff did when visiting a women's prison at the Federal Corrections Institution in Danbury, Connecticut—to connecting via email, phone, and face-to-face with individuals in need of personalized assistance, the Women For Hire Foundation offers guidance, information, and inspiration to support women at pivotal moments.

There is a tremendous strength that is growing in the world through sharing together, praying together, suffering together, and working together.

—MOTHER TERESA

As I watched the televised devastation caused by Hurricane Katrina, I felt compelled to do my part to assist. On Labor Day, 2005, I flew from New York to Houston and walked into the Astrodome with a handmade sign that read, "Are you looking for a job?" I was soon surrounded by people who shared their stories of struggle. They had lost everything. Their stories were similar, but one young woman named Doris Banks, a twenty-year-old single mother of a four-year-old boy, struck me with her innocence and fear.

Doris had been working at Taco Bell in New Orleans when the storm hit. She left her home, as it was overcome by floodwaters, and moved into the convention center, where she thought she'd reside for a night or two. Days later, to escape the horrendous conditions, she boarded a bus to Houston with nothing but the clothes on her back.

I called Taco Bell and learned that Doris was eligible for immediate rehire in Houston. She even got a raise. Doris later told me, "I didn't think my job could be transferred out here. I just thought I was going to lay hopeless."

I helped her secure government vouchers for housing assistance. Then I cross-referenced dozens of Taco Bell locations with apartment vacancies and found a nearby perfect match, since Doris doesn't drive. From there we filled many shopping carts with food, clothing, and life essentials, and Doris was on her way to rebuilding a life full of promise. She was shocked by what she called an "overwhelming blessing," and I remain in awe of my new friend's ability to rebound with determination. Doris believes she'll ultimately fulfill her dream to work in the medical field, where she will assist people just like she was assisted by me.

I've learned that I can't get someone a job or guarantee their success. I am able to guide them and enable them to see the possibilities. That's the beauty and reward of my work. Nothing makes me more proud personally or professionally than to play even a small role in witnessing another woman's success.

MAKE A DIFFERENCE TODAY

When we stop and help someone with his or her career and future, we make a huge impact. Imagine being the person who needs the help. How would you feel if someone stopped and generously assisted you? Sometimes a helping hand—a hand up, not a hand out—is all it takes to make a monumental difference.

CHAPTER 6

Caring about Kids and Kids Who Give Back

C hildren are our future. When we care about kids, we show the greatest possible degree of compassion. Children deserve to be cared for, to be safe, to be healthy, and to be nourished in body and soul. Yet sadly, as we all witness, this is often not the case.

When we help uplift a child, we lift up the entire family. Helping a child is simply the right thing to do. When we make a difference in one child's life, we make a difference in our own. Caring about kids also sets an example for everyone. The kindness and concern act as a continuum as these children experience the benefits and as they grow up. They are more likely to be candidates to continue the giving and give back. Some of the greatest lessons of all come from children. They seem to give effortlessly of themselves and for no other reason than they want to help and make a difference.

The entries in this chapter demonstrate a variety of causes that are dedicated to making a difference and are doing such amazing things for the benefit of children. The actions and organizations featured are made up of individuals who have found the greatest calling of all in life, reaching out and helping a child.

We salute these everyday heroes and organizations, along with all the extraordinary stories that are presented in this book. They are the backbone of goodness, and their devotion to strengthening and benefiting the lives of children is their greatest purpose.

GIVING KIDS A VOICE
Craig Kielburger, Founder and CEO, Free the Children

FreetheChildren.org

At twelve years old, Craig Kielburger demonstrated a level of compassion and vision that can only be called remarkable. With a million young people involved in education and development programs in forty-five countries, Free the Children, founded by Craig in 1995 when he was in middle school, is the world's largest network of children helping children through education. Craig first learned about the injustice of child labor by reading an article in the newspaper about a twelve-year-old boy from Pakistan who had been murdered for speaking out about the issue. Inspired to take action, he enlisted the help of friends to start a campaign that grew into one of the most important children's charities in the world. Inspired by his brother's passion and with his own interest in human rights, Craig's older brother, Marc Kielburger, a Harvard graduate, passed up the opportunity to pursue a career in investment banking to join the organization as Chief Executive Director.

Free the Children has built more than five hundred schools around the world. Its Adopt a Village model empowers children and their families in developing countries to break out of the cycle of poverty. The organization works to free children from poverty and exploitation, and, at the same time, to free children from the idea that they are powerless in the face of suffering. Through domestic empowerment programs and leadership training, it inspires youth to develop as socially conscious global citizens and become agents of change for their peers around the world.

When I approach a child, he inspires in me two sentiments: tenderness for what he is, and respect for what he may become.

—LOUIS PASTEUR

One day as I was paging through the newspaper looking for the comics, I came upon a story about a twelve-year-old child laborer who was killed when he tried to escape. The story and photograph made me so angry that I took them to my class and told my classmates I needed help! We gathered in my living room after school and read some other articles we researched, including one about a group of children marching through the streets of India crying, "We want freedom! Free the children!" We decided to name our organization Free The Children so that we could echo the voices of these exploited children.

Free The Children educates thousands of young people through school-based clubs and curriculums. We develop teacher training, hold stadium events, and sponsor summer camps that inspire and empower. As a result of what they learn, kids fundraise and adopt sister villages. In addition to the five hundred schools built by Free The Children, we've also launched 27,000 micro-economy cooperatives around the world. Each year, two thousand North

American kids volunteer overseas with us, building, teaching, and serving in our projects.

For us, the giving goes beyond charity. We're raising and inspiring a generation of kids to care. It's about the choices they make—from how they spend their time, to the clothes they wear, the food they eat, and the votes they cast. And it's about preparing them to pick careers that will make a difference. One of our latest initiatives is with the O Ambassadors campaign through Oprah Winfrey's Angel Network Foundation. We're helping to inspire a million kids across North America in two thousand schools to learn about global justice. Participating students come from every socioeconomic background, every part of the country, and every race and religion.

I've had the amazing fortune to sit down with the Dali Lama, to walk with Mother Teresa in Calcutta, and to meet with world leaders. But my greatest inspiration is the kids we work with! In Thailand I met an eight-year-old girl begging for food in the street, tapping her lips to indicate her hunger. So we handed her an orange, which she quickly tore apart. But when she looked up, a group of other hungry kids were staring at her longingly. Without a word, she walked over and opened up her hands so that they could share what she had been given. In Brazil I met a "family" of street kids, living on their own in a bus shelter and dressed in little more than newspaper. Jose, the fourteen-year-old head of the family, and I played soccer with a makeshift ball made of a cast-off water bottle—he had never seen or played with a real ball. When it was time to say goodbye, Jose insisted on giving me a gift. He literally took the shirt off his back, a soccer jersey from his favorite team. I tried to explain that I simply couldn't accept it, but he insisted. So I gave him the shirt I was wearing in return. I keep Jose's jersey framed on my bedroom wall. Yes, it's an honor to sit with royalty, but I think if the world were led by street children, there would be no more poverty.

When I started this, I didn't know I was going to start a charity. I just wanted to make it easier for other twelve-year-olds to make a difference. Now the next generation of twelve-year-olds is going to take this movement further than we could ever imagine!

MAKE A DIFFERENCE TODAY

Once you've found a way to give, share your passion with those closest to you. There's a wonderful sense of shared purpose when you involve those you love in your giving. When it comes to giving of themselves, young people can often be the inspiration for adults in a family. The lessons of giving are ageless.

THE SPIRIT OF THE DOLPHIN
Tom Tuohy, President and Founder, Dreams for Kids

DreamsForKids.org

Tom Tuohy has enough compassion to fill an ocean with kindness. Tuohy left a comfortable career as a lawyer to dedicate his life to his real passion—changing the lives of kids in need. Created by Tom to honor the hard-working aspirations of his own single mother, Dreams for Kids "inspires and empowers youth to fearlessly pursue their dreams and compassionately change the world." It all started on a cold Christmas Eve in 1989 when Tuohy and some friends brought Christmas to fifty-four homeless kids in a Chicago shelter who would not have had a holiday without them. The effort snowballed, becoming a nationwide, now global movement led by Tuohy and a small army of volunteers. Dreams for Kids continues to reach out to the homeless and underprivileged. Today, through a program known as Extreme Recess, it also promotes leadership and disability awareness and gives kids with disabilities the opportunity to participate in social and sports activities. The organization continues to be youth driven through its global Dream Leaders program, connecting diverse groups of youth to each other and to service in the world.

> *I shall pass through this world but once. Any good therefore that I can do or any kindness that I can show to any human being, let me do it now.*
>
> —MAHATMA GANDHI

My mother was a single parent who raised four children on her own. She soldiered on with such dignity, no matter how tough things got, and always with compassion for those who had less. She inspired me to look at what I could do to raise others up rather than at what was lacking in my life. I had to begin working at age twelve. Strengthened by my mom's example, I learned to look beyond any personal burden and focus on what I could give. As young children, my brothers and sister would join our mother, who worked two jobs and took public transportation, to deliver holiday meals to the elderly and bring gifts to those living in poverty. It is so important to have parents and mentors who inspire and empower children in their formative years. It shapes character. It creates strength and fuels passion.

A number of years ago, an extraordinary young man, Dick Marak, asked me to travel to Mexico with himself and his friend J.J. O'Connor. Five years prior, at age fifteen, J.J. was involved in a hockey accident that left him quadriplegic. One morning, J.J., Dick, and I decided to swim with the dolphins, something J.J. had always wanted to do. As the first dolphin circled the pool, she immediately stopped when she came to J.J. Anxious at first and obviously sensing a difference in him, she observed J.J. closely as she carefully began to approach him. We sensed something extraordinary was happening. As the dolphin reached J.J., she gently opened her fins, leaned in and kissed him! It was a moment I will never forget. I realized that dolphins are like most of us—a little bit nervous and uncertain around those with apparent disabilities, but having the capacity and privilege to reach out with compassion and the spirit of unconditional love. For J.J., seeing the dolphin accept him for who he is demonstrated the best that life has to offer. He told me the experience in Mexico was the most amazing thing that ever happened to him. I call that magical connection "the dolphin spirit." It inspired the title of my book, *Kiss of a Dolphin*, and it is this spirit that inspires us every day at *Dreams for Kids*.

Make a Difference Today

You don't have to wait to make a difference. You can change the world today with passion and a willingness to serve. We can embrace the possibilities of our world when we choose to see others from the inside out. Discovering what we have in common and celebrating our differences with acceptance, compassion, and love can transform lives, even our own.

MAKING WISHES COME TRUE
Peter Samuelson, Founder, Starlight Children's Foundation

Starlight.org

Peter Samuelson, a successful film and television producer in England, founded the Starlight Children's Foundation—an international charity serving over 2.4 million children annually and dedicated to lifting up the lives of seriously ill children and their families at a time of great stress. Since 1982, Starlight has grown to offer eight core psycho-social programs, each restoring some of the laughter, happiness, and self-esteem that serious illness takes away from kids and those who love them. After parents and health care providers confirmed the positive psychological and often medical impact of Starlight programming, in 1990 Peter brought together leaders including Steven Spielberg and General Norman Schwarzkopf to create the Starbright Foundation—a charity dedicated to developing media and technology-based programs to educate and empower children to cope with the medical, emotional and social challenges of their illness. In 2004, Starlight and Starbright completed a formal merger and became the Starlight Children's Foundation with offices throughout Australia, Canada, the United Kingdom, Japan, and across the United States. In 1999, Peter founded First Star, a separate national 501(c)(3) charity headquartered in Washington, D.C. that works to improve the public health, safety, and family life of America's abused and neglected children. With Peter as President, First Star provides "top-down" systemic leadership to increase quality and compassionate care for children within the child welfare system, basic civil and legal rights for every child, and safe, stable, and permanent homes for all children.

What we have done for ourselves alone dies with us; what we have done for others and the world remains and is immortal.

—ALBERT PIKE

In 1982, my cousin made me aware of a little boy with an inoperable brain tumor who was at a children's hospital in London. His one dream was to visit Disneyland. After consultation with his doctor and mother, we flew Sean and his mom to Disneyland. They and my cousin moved in with me for that two-week period in my condominium on Wilshire Boulevard in Los Angeles.

While in Los Angeles, we made sure he did all the things a child would enjoy and visited Disneyland and Knott's Berry Farm, and we even borrowed a friend's helicopter and pilot, and overall we tried to create the trip of a lifetime. However, Sean was seriously ill. Though he returned to London with his Disney sweatshirt and Mickey Mouse ears, Sean died a few months later.

The epiphany came to me weeks later when I was having a business lunch with a Senior Executive with HBO. As a film and television producer, I was trying to sell him a project. He didn't buy it, but as we were lunching and still eating the salad, he asked, "What's new and exciting in your life?" And so I shared with him that this amazing thing had just happened to me and affected me a great deal: I told him the story of Sean.

He was so affected by the story that he began to cry. As we sat there, he just wept, big tears rolling down his face. I remember vividly how the poor man had to leave the table to collect himself. After lunch I went on my way back to my office, and as I was standing in the elevator, I thought how powerful this story had been to me, but that I hadn't known it would be so powerful to a total stranger.

Inspired by Sean, I conceived of an organization that would help grant the wishes of other children like him. That's how the Starlight Foundation was born. From little acorns grow big oak trees!

Make a Difference Today

Apply your talents to the needs. Peter Samuelson used his talents for entertainment to create an organization to improve the lives of millions of seriously ill children, bringing laughter and joy into their world. A personal experience led to the development of an international organization; look into your own community and find new, personal ways to make a difference. Big things start small!

GIVING BACK, ONE ON ONE
Judy Vredenburgh, President and CEO,
Big Brothers, Big Sisters of America

BigBrothersBigSisters.org

Big Brothers Big Sisters positively impacts American children's lives, making a measurable difference through caring, consistent relationships that have a direct and lasting impact on communities. The mission is to help children reach their potential through professionally supported, one-to-one mentoring relationships that make a measurable difference. President and CEO Judy Vredenburgh has helped the organization grow in nationwide revenue from $183 million in 2000 to $274 million in 2006. In less than a decade under Judy's passionate leadership, Big Brothers Big Sisters has more than doubled the number of children served to 242,000 from 118,000.

> *If you care about kids, you can be an advocate, you can be a donor, you can rally others, but what you can't do is nothing.*

> — JUDY VREDENBURGH

The need is great! We need sustainable quality along with increased revenue to sustain matches over time. With the growing numbers of Little Brothers and Sisters, there is an increasing need to have more participation. My personal experience started with a typical adolescent named Sherice, my Little Sister. She was twelve years old and naturally smart, but suddenly doing poorly in school. At first, we didn't connect until I took her to a museum that was featuring a collection of African American art, which Sherice loved. That was the special moment when our relationship changed, and Sherice began to open up as we began a special friendship.

What we achieve through the quality relationships Big Brothers Big Sisters has fostered for more than a hundred years is the real strength behind our success. Volunteer Big Brothers or Big Sisters get just as much out of the experience as the Littles do. They are shared experiences that are relationship driven. The deep friendships cultivate into something transformational that is unique to each volunteer match.

The little moments lead to big magic, help open doors and span horizons for young people. The mentors show children what is possible that they may not have known about. "When Little Brothers and Little Sisters feel good about themselves, they positively impact their friends and families, their schools, and their communities. These young people believe in themselves because a Big Brother or Big Sister believed in them."

We have placed attention on measurable impacts from Big Brothers Big Sisters mentoring. We implemented a service delivery model supported by a technology system that enables measurement of every aspect of the Big Brothers Big Sisters mentoring programs. Having an integrated database with all of the volunteer matches and keeping connections is critical. Performance management is the marketing tool to keep relationships solid.

Big Brothers Big Sisters helps children reach their potential through professionally supported one-to-one mentoring with measurable results. Little Brothers and Sisters, as they're called, are 46 percent less likely to begin using illegal drugs, 27 percent less likely to begin using alcohol, and 52 percent less likely to skip school. In addition, they are more confident in their schoolwork performance and able to get along better with their families. The organization has helped prevent young people from getting involved in gangs, crime, and drug abuse. Kids benefit from our mentoring relationships throughout their adult lives: they are more likely to graduate from high school and further their education in trade schools and college. The relationship is essential in expanding opportunities for a successful life.

Currently, Big Brothers Big Sisters is trying to strengthen our stature and gain more influence with the purpose of bringing in more resources for the kids and families. While we encourage caring adults who represent a range of professions to be Bigs, we also collaborate with celebrities and high-profile individuals to get involved. Troy Aikman, Hill Harper, and Laura Bush have all offered their time and support to help our cause.

The beauty of the organization is that anybody can be a part of the movement. If you care about kids, you can be an advocate, you can be a donor, you can rally others, but what you can't do is nothing. Opening doors will show what is possible. We welcome everyone.

MAKE A DIFFERENCE TODAY

Mentoring a child is one of the most rewarding experiences you can have. Sharing your time, experiences, and wisdom lets children know they matter. Combine your interests with their curiosity—fish together, bake together, take a hike, make a difference.

THE GIFT OF EDUCATION
Ben Maddox, Teacher, with Wendy Kopp, Founder,
Teach for America

TeachforAmerica.org

Wendy Kopp founded Teach For America as a national corps of outstanding college graduates and professionals who commit two years to teach in urban and rural public schools and become leaders in the effort to expand educational opportunity. The program has become one of the nation's largest providers of teachers for low-income communities and is recognized for building a pipeline of committed leaders. This year, 6,200 Teach for America corps members are reaching over 400,000 students in low-income communities across the country. They join thousands of Teach For America alumni who are assuming significant leadership roles in education. Last year, Teach For America attracted more than 24,000 top college graduates and accepted 20 percent of these applicants into the corps.

One day, all children in this nation will have the opportunity to attain an excellent education.

—TEACH FOR AMERICA VISION

"Maclovio, why don't you have a phone number?" "Consuelo, why can't you come to Saturday school?" "Anthony, if you don't come for morning tutoring you won't be able to attend the tenth grade." The atmosphere is intense: fifteen-year-old girls fight constantly over boys; students deal drugs during lunch, and one of my special education students even brought a weapon to school. I'm in the Rio Grande Valley, the southern section of the Texas-Mexico border that encompasses two of the four poorest counties in the United States—I live and teach in one of those counties.

Why would I put myself in such a difficult situation with hardly any teaching experience? And all in an environment that lacks the academic rigor or supportive environment in which I grew up? The answer lies in my commitment to serving others and to give back what has been essentially given to me—an excellent education. I joined Teach for America not only to challenge myself professionally but also to help remedy the educational achievement gap that exists in our country today. Maclovio, Consuelo, and Anthony are why I teach for America.

As one of the most influential people according to *Time Magazine* in 2008, Wendy Kopp's dream of creating a national service teacher corps has now become a reality. As a college senior, Wendy proposed Teach For America's (TFA) creation in her Princeton University undergraduate thesis. Wendy believed that student leaders might make a difference and now, nineteen years later, TFA has proved that a combination of leaders with head, heart, and soul can change our schools with nearly 3,700 new recruits this year.

Initially, Wendy raised $2.5 million in start-up funding and launched a grass-roots recruitment campaign. During TFA's first year in 1990, 500 young people taught in six low-income communities across the country. Since then, TFA's influential network has grown to over 20,000. There are more than 400,000 students impacted annually and nearly 3 million students reached since TFA's inception.

In an interview with Charlie Rose, Wendy said, "What can I do for my life [after graduation]? I answered it with Teach for America." TFA exists to eliminate educational inequity by enlisting our nation's most promising future leaders in the effort.

With 13 million children locked into poverty, an attainable, quality education is difficult to reach. Teach for America believes that there is a way to solve the problem, and it starts with ambitious, goal-oriented teachers. TFA has seen evidence in classrooms where kids can excel when they are given the opportunities they deserve. TFA looks for exceptional leaders as teachers who have a track record of achievement, perseverance, and outstanding leadership skills. Corps members are goal oriented, persistent, and give everything to overcome obstacles. Corps members must have a desire to work relentlessly, and the challenges they face in making a significant impact on their students' academic achievement are immense.

In Houston, there are about two hundred high-performing charter schools, mostly inspired by TFA alums. Michelle Rhee is Washington, D.C.'s new Chancellor for public schools. Her deputy and 10 percent of her team are TFA alums.

TFA recruits the best and the brightest and connects with the neediest. With a bold strategic plan and recruitment at more than five hundred colleges and universities, TFA is gaining momentum in the political and policy world. The experience in TFA is not only transformative for teachers but also transformative for the students.

MAKE A DIFFERENCE TODAY

We all have some skill or expertise that we can teach someone else. From being a role model to sharing a particular skill, give to others by sharing your know how. Spread your gratitude by thanking a teacher or someone who has taught you something that has helped you in your life. Let him or her know how much their efforts mattered. Unless you give the gift of appreciation, they may never know.

GIVING LOW-INCOME TEENS
A DIFFERENT CHOICE
Julie Kantor, Vice President, National Foundation for Teaching Entrepreneurship

NFTE.com

The National Foundation for Teaching Entrepreneurship (NFTE) is a nonprofit organization that teaches teens from low-income communities to become entrepreneurs. By transferring street smarts into business smarts, the program gives youth a creative, productive outlet and builds skills that can change adult lives.

The program was started by Steve Mariotti in 1988. Mariotti left corporate America to work as a special education teacher in some of New York City's most challenging communities. He watched and learned from the students, then decided to re-enter the business world with a twist, building a 'mini-MBA' curriculum for at-risk teens. To date, NFTE has reached some 186,000 young people in twenty-one states and thirteen countries. The program teaches teens from low-income communities viable alternatives to unemployment and low-paying jobs.

Julie Silard Kantor, NFTE National Vice President, has taught entrepreneurship to urban youth since 1992. As NFTE's Executive Director in Massachusetts and then Washington D.C. for fifteen years, she has been fully engaged in every level of the organization, from teaching classes at public school and youth programs to recruiting staff, teachers, and increasing the program's visibility among business and community leaders. In her new role on a national level, she will focus on the advancement of the adoption and expansion of entrepreneurship education in the nation's schools as a way of engaging young people from low income communities in academic performance and arresting the nation's dropout rate.

We are each of us an angel with one wing; we can only fly by embracing each other.

—UNKNOWN

I first met Steve in 1991 when I basically snuck into a conference that my department usually didn't attend by offering to take pictures. I was with *Inc.* magazine at the time and volunteered to take photos and market videos so I could listen in. What I heard and saw was a bunch of incredibly energetic teenagers running around; I was immediately drawn to them. TJ, a confident sixteen-year-old, handed me a business card and told me that, while I looked nice in my navy suit, I wasn't well accessorized! I learned that this young man had launched his own successful scarf business. His persuasive manner and charming personality led me to buy two on the spot. He then proceeded to show me his business plan, his ideas for beating the competition, and his annual income statement. To say the least, I was impressed.

I learned that his business acumen had come from NFTE's "mini MBA" program. I also learned that TJ was not just having fun; he was the chief breadwinner for his family. As I took my seat, I listened as Steve told his amazing story. He owned an import/ export company in New York City and one day while jogging was mugged by a group of teens. As he lay in a hospital bed, he tried to understand what was going on with them, why violence over $5 or $10? Then and there he decided to become a teacher, and he worked in the roughest neighborhoods of New York City. He saw that kids were not learning anything about business except typing, so he decided to fill the gap. He ultimately sold his business so he could devote himself to helping kids develop skills and self-esteem that would let them become "presidents or owners of their own lives," as he likes to say.

I was barely twenty-two years old at the time and had always been supported by people who believed in me and my dreams. I was blown away by Steve's story, and I decided to volunteer with NFTE. The values resonated deeply with me—my father was a Holocaust survivor and had come to this country from Budapest to realize the dream of owning a home and being able to go to college. He has lived the American Dream! I went to work for NFTE and have trained thousands of kids and teachers across the globe. These beautiful kids are so worth the effort! They are America's future leaders, and they're realizing that high school is relevant to their economic futures and becoming more engaged in school. They have the will to succeed! One of our students, Michelle Araujo, whom I met in 1991, said it best: "My dream is not to die in poverty, but to have poverty die in me."

MAKE A DIFFERENCE TODAY

The best way to ensure that you make good on your good intentions to help others is to develop a system of accountability. Promise yourself weekly or monthly involvement with kids, seniors, shut-ins, or others in need of what you have to give. And absolutely refuse to break that promise. The more you do, the more you'll want to do.

DANNY THOMAS'S DREAM
KEEPS ON GIVING
*John P. Moses, CEO, ALSAC/St. Jude Children's
Research Hospital*

StJude.org

Imagine a hospital without a patient billing department. The reason is simple: At St. Jude Children's Research Hospital in Memphis, all patients accepted are treated without any costs or regard to the family's ability to pay. St. Jude has revolutionized everything about the way children with cancer and other catastrophic diseases are treated. With research and patient care under one roof, St. Jude is a miracle in motion.

Opened in 1962 in Memphis, St. Jude was the dream of Danny Thomas. Born in Deerfield, Michigan, in 1912, Danny grew up listening to stories told by his elders. The stories inspired in him a desire to entertain, but opportunities were few. As a young adult, Danny found himself on his knees in a church praying to St. Jude Thaddeus, the patron saint of hopeless causes. "Show me my way in life, and I will build you a shrine," he vowed. In fact, Danny became one of the biggest names in show business with his series, *Make Room for Daddy*. But success did not cloud his vision. Danny searched for and found a way to honor his promise. It was St. Jude, a research hospital dedicated to finding cures for the sickest of children. Within a decade of its opening, St Jude had raised the cure rate for one form of childhood leukemia from 4 percent to 50 percent. Danny believed show business was a vehicle to permit him to fulfill his destiny, and he worked tirelessly for the hospital until he died in 1991. Today, ALSAC, the fundraising organization for St. Jude, is America's second-largest health care charity, ensuring that St. Jude continues to be a place where revolutionary discoveries happen every day. Amazingly, a new scientific study is published every seventeen hours!

John Moses became CEO of ALSAC in 2005, promising to continue to work toward the day Danny Thomas dreamed of, when "no child should die in the dawn of life." Moses is an attorney who served as Special Counsel to the Pennsylvania House of Representatives and Chair of the ALSAC Board of Directors.

Success in life has nothing to do with what you gain in life or accomplish for yourself. It's what you do for others.

—DANNY THOMAS

When Danny founded ALSAC in 1957, it took five years to raise the first $1.25 million. Today, our costs are about $1.3 million per day! That's because of our unsurpassed, all-expenses-paid patient and family care, including transportation, food, and all related medical costs, as well as our unparalleled scientific research. Danny often told me, "When a child is sick, the family suffers." So while we have only about 75 beds, we treat some 200 to 250 children a day, most of whom are able to spend the night out of the hospital with their own families in comfortable surroundings like the Memphis Grizzlies House and Target House. Danny always wanted to make sure that the only thing parents had to think about was the health of their children.

One of our missions is public awareness and education. So on any given day, it's likely that you'll see at least one celebrity taking a tour along with other interested citizens. We've had the Duchess of York, Robin Williams, Julie Andrews, Bono, and so many others. Sure, their presence means a great deal, but they never overshadow our patients. I'll never forget when I was first named Chairman of the hospital, I asked one of our security guards if he could drive me to the airport. "Mr. Moses, I'm sorry, but I can't do that today." When I asked why he answered, "Well, sir, my pal Jimmy is having his last chemo treatment, and I promised him I wouldn't miss it!"

One telling story comes to mind. Mary, the grandmother of twelve-year-old Daniel, heard Marlo Thomas, Danny's daughter, speaking on the *Today Show* about St. Jude. She perked up as Marlo described debilitating symptoms of a rare brain cancer known as ATRT. They sounded much like those experienced by her grandson, Daniel, who had been told by countless doctors that there was no hope for him. The family immediately contacted St. Jude, and within days of being accepted, Daniel and his mother were on their way to Memphis for treatment. Their eight-month stay included extensive treatment and therapies.

Afterward, as Daniel was a few weeks from going home, when he was asked how he felt about St. Jude this remarkable, wise-beyond-his-years young man answered from the depths of his heart: "St. Jude gave me my life back. Every penny donated here is worth millions."

Those who donate are equally extraordinary. An example is Joan and Arnold Weiss of Memphis and Palm Beach, who are the founders of the St. Jude Children's Research Hospital Gala in Palm Beach. When they realized that St. Jude did not have a gala in the Palm Beach area, they sprang into action and established it. At one of the events, the Weiss's successfully bid at a St. Jude gala for a painting by Gustavo, a young patient from Venezuela. The next day they received a phone call from St. Jude informing them that Gustavo wanted to meet the people who had purchased his artwork. They happily went to the hospital to meet Gustavo, who cried when he saw the stuffed dog they carried with them. It was identical to pictures of the dog Gustavo's family had left in Venezuela when they came to the United States for treatment. They became close to Gustavo and hosted a birthday party for him. When they told him he could invite anyone he wanted, he chose his St. Jude doctors. Today, the families remain connected, and Joan and Arnold do all they can to help spread the word about St. Jude.

Make a Difference Today

When you hear of a family facing challenges due to illness, there are many ways to reach out. These include sharing information or researching resources, or gathering your community to offer financial, emotional, or logistical support. Bring a meal, or organize a schedule for neighbors to deliver meals to the home. Offer to take other children to sports and other activities. Offer to mow the lawn, shovel snow, or shop for groceries. Such gestures show what matters most—how much you care.

A FIELD OF DREAMS FOR STUDENTS
Della Britton Baeza, President and CEO, Jackie Robinson Foundation

JackieRobinson.org

At a time before philanthropy was what it is today, we learned through baseball legend Jackie Robinson how one could make a difference beyond writing a check. Aside from the impact Jackie Robinson made during his lifetime, in 1973, the year after Jackie passed away, Rachel Robinson, his wife, founded The Jackie Robinson Foundation to continue to positively influence American society, invoking his name and the values for which he stood. The foundation provides generous financial assistance to college students, but perhaps more importantly, it provides extensive mentoring and career and personal development strategies that promote not only success but also excellence among its student constituents. The foundation subscribes to the motto that "A life is not important except in the impact it has on other lives." Fittingly, that statement will appear in the atrium at Citi Field, which is the New York Mets' new stadium in New York City, in memory of Jack Robinson, who dedicated his life to making a difference.

A life is not important except in the impact it has on other lives.

—JACKIE ROBINSON.

During Jackie Robinson's era, the salaries in professional sports were not what they are today. Nonetheless, when he retired from baseball, Jackie Robinson unselfishly gave his time as a celebrity. He worked extensively with young people and advocated on behalf of equal opportunity and social justice, believing that people would heed the message of someone who had displayed the courage, talent, and tenacity to break down the barriers that divided the nation. Indeed, in 1947, when Jackie Robinson played his first baseball game for the Brooklyn Dodgers, he not only integrated major league baseball and the mainstream of professional sports in America, but he arguably broke the color barrier in society generally and thereby set the tone for the modern civil rights era. Dr. Martin Luther King referred to him as "a freedom rider before freedom rides" and often publicly thanked Jackie Robinson for his great impact on American society.

In keeping with the spirit and values embodied in how Jackie Robinson lived his life, the Jackie Robinson Foundation supports deserving, motivated, and financially challenged students throughout their college careers and, in turn, requires these hundreds of students to perform community service work during their tenure as Jackie Robinson Scholars. The belief is that once service becomes part of their lives while enrolled in the foundation's program, they will go on to embrace the concept and incorporate it into their independent adult lives as well.

What are some of the observations that we at the Jackie Robinson Foundation have made in our philanthropic efforts? Philanthropy is an art form. Because the landscape is so full, a donor has to be wise in giving money away, and the recipients of philanthropy have to be disciplined in prudently using the money given to them. In the words of Warren Buffet, "It takes a lot of time, energy, and wisdom to give [money] away intelligently with the greatest impact."

We are finding more and more that, because of the range and sheer quantity of organized philanthropic causes today, people give to people perhaps more often than they give to the cause itself. That is, people most often give to somebody they know or like in an effort to distinguish among the myriad of worthy charitable causes and to assure themselves that appropriate due diligence has been done on the worthiness of the cause by someone they respect and trust.

There indeed has been a proliferation of nonprofit organizations over the past decade or so. In New York, for example, the number of nonprofit entities registered with the State has increased by 150 percent in the last ten years. Nonprofit fundraising has become tremendously competitive, and while giving has increased exponentially as well, the process of raising charitable funds now requires sophistication, diligence, and a well-honed set of skills, including donor cultivation, marketing, and accountability assurance. The culture of giving is thriving, however, and has seeped into mainstream society. It is now politically and socially correct to talk about what one is doing oneself and what others are doing to help those less fortunate. The well-paid athletes and celebrities of today are expected to support charitable causes, and that bodes well for the increased challenges of raising money and attracting highly skilled staff to manage nonprofit organizations.

And, regardless of the motivation for giving, it is clear that once a donor is engaged, their commitment becomes emotional and mutually satisfying and is reinforced through the reality of the impact that it has on others. As Oprah Winfrey professed at the dedication ceremony of the Oprah Winfrey Leadership Academy for Girls in South Africa, "I started off thinking it was something for you, but you have given me so much more." We find that to be the case on a daily basis once our donors meet the incredible young people whom they help through our program.

MAKE A DIFFERENCE TODAY

Writing a check is not the only way to give, although it is a vital part of philanthropy to be sure. Consider mentoring a young person through sports. Volunteer in a book fair for impoverished school systems. Write legislators and advocate on behalf of worthy causes. You do not always need a lot of experience. To make a difference, you need only to genuinely care and to "do your homework." The good you do will come back many times over.

ONE MOVE AT A TIME
Orrin Hudson, Founder, Be Someone, Inc.

BeSomeone.Org

Air Force Veteran and former state trooper Orrin Hudson started a crime prevention program called Be Someone, Inc. and is a recipient of numerous awards including the Martin Luther King Jr. Community Service award, National Self-Esteem award, and the Educator of the Year award. On May 24, 2000, he walked away from his business and started a crime prevention charter education program to teach young-adults to think it out instead of shooting it out and push pawns on a chessboard instead of drugs. He believes, "Evil prevails when good people do nothing," so Orrin started Be Someone, Inc. and is on a mission to make this world a better place. He does this by showing young adults the beauty of chess and how to think three moves ahead.

A man wrapped up in himself makes a very small bundle.

—BENJAMIN FRANKLIN

It's a real breath of fresh air to teach young adults the challenging game of chess and how to think. That focus and determined direction and concentration is everything. I've seen firsthand kids' lives changed by having a talent, the ability to think things out, and to make better use of their time. I received the gift of the love of the game of chess when I first met James Edger (a white teacher in an all black high school) when I was at Hayes High School in 1978. He tutored me for four years and provided me with a bigger and more powerful perspective on the game but also on the game of life.

Now I pay it forward everyday, teaching kids what was shared to me. While we are playing we get to know each other, and kids learn the power of their thinking and that there are other productive and meaningful ways to spend free time. My vision to change the world in a positive way begins with one move at a time.

MAKE A DIFFERENCE TODAY

What move can you make? Teaching kids to play chess or learn a new skill or talent may not seem like such a significant move, but sharing your talents could change many lives, giving meaning and a fresh sense of hope and possibility. Examine the board or field or arena in front of you and make your move.

PLAYING THE GAME OF LIFE ...
AND WINNING
Neil Phillips, Head, Upper School, Landon School

1on1basketball.com

As one of the few Harvard University students to ever play both football and basketball, Neil Phillips gave his all in the field and in the classroom. Since graduating, he has been devoted to educating and inspiring young people, primarily through athletics. In 1994 Neil created One on One Basketball, a skill- and life-coaching program that's reached 15,000 young players nationally and abroad. He also worked for two sports-based nonprofit organizations, including the Positive Coaching Alliance, which seeks to "transform youth sports so sports can transform youth." In 2003, Neil joined the faculty of the Landon School, a private boys' school in Bethesda, Maryland, and in 2005 was named Head of the Upper School. He is a tireless advocate for helping kids reach their potential by reaching beyond themselves.

> *Treat people as if they were what they ought to be, and help them become what they are capable of being.*
>
> —GOETHE

Selflessness—the idea of sublimating one's personal betterment for the interests and needs of the larger group—can be a tough concept for young people, mostly due to their stage of development.

My goal is to get kids to care about something or someone other than themselves. I want them to *always* envision themselves as givers, not just when they're doing a community service project or attending a charitable event. As a coach, I've always emphasized that the group means more than any individual in it. Once kids get this, it leads to incredible personal growth. The students I'm working with now are in a high-stress, competitive academic environment that can contribute to some real self-centeredness. But what happens when you take the *you* out of the equation and think about the *we*? That's my focus.

In the late 1990s, through One on One Basketball, we ran a series of basketball camps in tiny towns and villages in Bosnia. We loaded a plane with volunteers and donated shoes, shirts, and caps. It was an effort to repair some of the damage that had been done to kids caught up in a series of Balkan wars. We taught skills, but we taught character development, too, and it was an extraordinary experience. I remember in one town we met a young girl who was hesitant about participating. She was shy, she had no idea how to play basketball, and understandably, she was distrustful of strangers. Reluctantly, she joined us.

At the end of the three-day camp, she walked up to me with her mom and looked hard at me for a minute, then reached up and gave me a huge hug. There were no words exchanged; our tears did the talking. We had managed to reach this girl despite all the trials she'd been through.

MAKE A DIFFERENCE TODAY

It's said that you can judge the heart of a society by how it treats its elderly. But you can also judge by how a society treats its young. Youth have inherent energy and wonderment and optimism—and they haven't lived long enough to become skeptical. They are ambassadors for ideals, optimism, and action. Find ways to help harness their incredible power for all the good it can do. Reach out to a young person you believe in today.

ADOPTING A NEW VIEW OF GIVING
Randi Thompson, Co-Founder
and CEO/Executive Director, Kidsave

Kidsave.org

Randi Thompson was a successful public relations and social marketing consultant when she ran headlong into a world she never knew existed. Her business partner, Terry Baugh, adopted a baby in Russia and told Thompson about the deplorable conditions she found in Russian orphanages. Thompson, also an adoptive parent, wanted to see for herself. While working on a health promotion project in Kazakhstan, she visited a local orphanage and was changed forever by what she discovered. Forgotten children, especially those who were older and considered harder to adopt, were being warehoused with little hope for a brighter future. Thompson and Baugh decided to devote their life's work to helping older, overlooked children find loving families. They created Kidsave in 1997 which, since that time, has made more than 2,700 family connections and permanent placements.

The organization works on several levels. It brings children living in orphanages to the United States for summer visits during which they stay with host/advocates and also operates a year-round family visit program for older U.S. foster kids on weekends. These volunteer hosts are people who may be interested in adopting themselves or who, through their own social networking, help

Kidsave shine a light on kids who otherwise wouldn't have a chance for a permanent family. Kidsave is also building local capacity in Russia and Colombia, and operating family visit and mentoring programs on the ground. Through its advocacy initiatives, Kidsave created the Families for Orphans Coalition and is working to transform child welfare systems.

> *Do all the good you can, and make as little fuss about it as possible.*

> —CHARLES DICKENS

When you ask someone if they can help the 33 million kids in the world living without families, they can't begin to imagine what they can do. But when you talk about the possibility of reaching out to one orphan or foster child, it's a very different story. Suddenly you've empowered someone to give a child the possibility of a future filled with love and success. Once people get involved as volunteer advocates, they want to do more and more.

When we started focusing on who was really out there helping these forgotten kids we learned about a few scattered efforts, but nobody was systematically attacking the problem. Once they emancipated or aged out of the child welfare system these kids ended up on the streets—homeless, jobless, and in many cases turning to crime and prostitution to survive. Terry and I started by donating our marketing services to the effort, but it soon became clear that more was needed. So we decided to give up our day jobs and start Kidsave with a little grant funding and a lot of hope.

That first summer we worked with placement agencies to bring 177 kids from Russia and Kazakhstan to the United States for a six-week summer visit; they were nearly all adopted. That became our Summer Miracles Program, which has found permanent families for more than 90 percent of the kids who participate and is Kidsave's family visit model. Host families not only feed, house, and mentor children, they also help raise funds, organize events, and advocate for adoption in their communities. We have only about twenty people on staff in the United States and a handful in the other countries we serve. But a great deal of our work is done by incredible volunteers. I call Kidsave the little engine that could!

We are also working to get individuals and governments to focus on this enormous, worldwide problem. When we started working in Colombia in 2003, we talked to government leaders and explained that lasting change would occur only if the child welfare system was committed to finding connections for these kids inside Colombia, too. Today, we've placed about 250 Colombian orphans in U.S. families and partner with the government to place kids in host families in Colombia. Our ultimate goal is to turn these programs over to local activists, and that's starting to happen. The Sakhalin, Russia, community was able to close three orphanages after two years of involvement with Kidsave!

MAKE A DIFFERENCE TODAY

Everybody has the capacity—in their hearts, their homes or through work—to demonstrate concern for others. There are countless ways to share what we have with those who, through no fault of their own, are in need. Social networking, talking to others and becoming a source of information, is an enormously important way to help. Between family, friends, and colleagues, the number of contacts most people have is quite large. Use those connections for the greater good.

CELEBRATING LIFE BY GIVING TO OTHERS
Kate Atwood, Founder, Kate's Club

KatesClub.org

Kate's Club is an Atlanta nonprofit whose mission is to empower children and teens facing life after the death of a parent or sibling. Founded by Kate Atwood, who lost her mother at the age of twelve, Kate's Club provides recreational, social, and emotional grief support to all school-age children helping them navigate through their grief journey. Kate's Club takes a traumatic experience and unites children from all backgrounds who share a similar experience to help create a community of support.

> *Death leaves a heartache no one can heal; love leaves a memory no one can steal.*
>
> —FROM A HEADSTONE IN IRELAND

At Kate's Club, we understand that children grieve differently than adults. By surrounding them with peer support, engaging programs, and committed volunteers and staff, kids feel safe to share their struggles and have a place to begin their healing. Kate's Club has become a haven for kids where they can have fun, be kids, share their stories, and gain the skills they need to lead happy and healthy lives. Each of our children is an individual, but when they come together they create a world where it is okay to grieve. The impact of one person at Kate's Club is simple; when any one of us reaches out to help someone in need, the reward is the sense of peace we feel when we have helped make life easier, better, or more hope-filled for someone else.

Our greatest success at Kate's Club is heard in the voice of our children. Grief isn't a challenge that everyone can see, it is very much beholden to the individual who carries it. When our children feel safe enough to share their stories, we are victorious in our efforts to support them. I remember participating in a support group in which we were closing our group with a question and answer session. One little girl chose a question that I can never forget: "When does it end?" "It" is what everyone who has lost a parent or sibling is hoping will go away—the feelings of hurt, pain, missing your loved one, being angry, being scared, feeling guilty or alone. I wanted to know the answer myself, and being the adult in the room, I felt obliged to answer, but I hesitated. One of the little girls in our group filled the void wisely when she offered, "It may not ever end, but it does get easier."

We live in a culture where grief is seen as something we can fix. We can fix everything else, so why can't we fix grief? We shouldn't aim to fix it, nor the children who experience it. They don't need to be fixed; they need our support. At Kate's Club, support is what we offer, and the children often find their support and the answers to tough questions from their peers. Without being fully aware, they are giving the gift of support and creating a community where they can begin the healing process. There is no goal line in grief, but with the right support, our children can still be victorious throughout their lives.

I believe it is profoundly more powerful to give when you yourself are struggling. The feeling of fulfillment and purpose when you do help someone ends up helping you too. That's one of the magical things that happens at Kate's Club. Our kids, who are all facing the hardships of grief, walk a path together and ultimately reward themselves through helping someone else. I believe if we all reach beyond our own hardships and extend compassion to someone else, we all win in the end. When you give, you truly live.

Make a Difference Today

Losses in our own lives can lead us to greater compassion. Think of your own life—setbacks, challenges, even tragedies. What have they taught you? How have you grown from them? What can you do with the power they have given you? How can you give that power back to others?

Chapter 7

A Community of Giving

Community is the framework that gives purpose to our world. It ranges from our next-door neighbors to alliances that provide formal support systems. Community embraces us on so many meaningful levels. Community makes us feel cared for and part of something more important and bigger than any one of us.

Whether you have made a difference in your own local backyard or reached out across the ocean of needs around the world, when we bond together we strengthen our giving. Ironically, we never know when we'll be on the other side of the equation and be the receiver. Yet, communities are created all over the world, and it's because of these unified groups of people dedicated to a common cause that we can accomplish so much. It's this bonded group of givers who rise to the occasion to help make the world a better place.

A dedicated volunteer named Betty Sunshine sheds light on giving around the world and says, "Some believe philanthropy is the act of giving to others. I believe philanthropy is the greatest gift you can give to yourself. We are here, not to exist in isolation, but to connect, and create community in our midst. Not engaging in the experience is a deprivation. When you indulge yourself by repairing the world, one charitable act at a time; you know the feeling of caring, making a difference, and leaving a legacy."

In this chapter, which addresses a community of giving, the idea of coming together is so important. We see how organizations and individuals have sewn together the thread of caring into a blanket of warmth and endless support. We witness firsthand love in action as people join their hands and their voices with hope to help others rise above their circumstances. It's amazing how great the parts of a whole are when they combine their talents, treasures, and time to create something larger than themselves. It's that feeling of community that lets us rejoice in a world that dares enough to care.

GIVE UNITED, LIVE UNITED
Brian Gallagher, President and CEO,
United Way of America

LiveUnited.org

With annual support topping an astounding $4 billion, the United Way system is the largest nonprofit in the United States. A global giving network encompassing forty-seven countries and 1,287 U.S. organizations, United Way has worked for more than one hundred years to mobilize the caring power of communities to make a difference in individual lives. United Way brings together people from across the community—in government, business, nonprofits, labor, faith groups, and ordinary citizens to tackle big issues. Because when a child succeeds in school, when a family becomes financially stable, and when people are in good health, everybody wins. The organization was launched in 1887 when a Denver priest, two ministers, and a rabbi came together to address the welfare issues of their city. More than one hundred twenty years later, the organization is focused on advancing the common good by creating opportunities for a better life through education, income, and health.

Brian Gallagher is a career veteran of United Way who became President and CEO in 2002, immediately taking on the challenge of leading the transformation of the organization to focus on community impact. Today, the organization collaborates with partners from all sectors to address community issues, a striking evolution from its former role as a raiser and distributor of funds.

Gallagher measures success by the impact achieved—lives changed and communities shaped—through programs like United Way Financial Stability Partnership. It empowers lower income individuals and families by providing them with knowledge and tools to increase their personal income, savings, and assets.

Be an opener of doors for such as come after thee.

—RALPH WALDO EMERSON

People are energized by hope. I think for too long in this sector, we've tried to motivate people by telling them how bad things are for others. In my experience, it's better instead to talk about how good things can be and to give people an immediate way to get involved. Today we're seeing large-scale change in the role of our institutions, a redefinition of the social contract. In the old industrial economy there were clear roles: government was the safety net, business created jobs for anyone with a high school education, and where there were gaps, nonprofits stepped in to fill them. But all that's changing—we're a global knowledge economy that requires advanced education. And government can't do what it once did.

I had a rather chaotic childhood and found refuge at the home of a friend whose parents helped me discover sports and eventually helped me focus on getting to college. I was the first in my family to go to college. That experience helped me realize that none of us is autonomous—the price of our independence is our interdependence. And that's certainly true for communities. It's time we proclaim our interdependence and create solutions that will encourage long-term human success. United Way is not an institution, but a community resource to help us identify those solutions.

When it comes to giving, we're still an incredibly generous society. But people increasingly want to make a difference about an issue or cause. And that has ignited social movements that result in change—civil rights, women's rights, or a ban on public smoking. People are no longer content to write checks; they want to get personally involved in causes so that they can make a difference. But there's so much yet to do—we have to deal with the 47 million people who lack access to health insurance, and we have one of the widest income gaps since the 1920s. There's great motivation to help another individual, but we also have to deal with the root causes that put many people in this country at risk. It takes social networking to put that kind of pressure on policy makers.

MAKE A DIFFERENCE TODAY

Volunteer your time to help improve education by becoming a mentor in your local school district. Invest in your community by contributing to a cause like financial stability for lower-income working families. Raise your voice to champion an issue like health care access by writing to your congressional representative.

GIVING OPPORTUNITY
Jeannette Yeunyul Pai-Espinosa, President, Crittenton
FoundationCrittentonFoundation.org

The National Crittenton Foundation has a 125-year legacy of supporting the empowerment of vulnerable girls and young women. At the heart of today's Crittenton Foundation is "a passionate commitment to, and belief in the will and strength of at-risk and system-involved girls, young women, and their families to reach their potential." In 1883, the first Florence Crittenton Home opened in New York City to serve "lost and fallen women and wayward young women." It was founded by Charles Crittenton to honor the memory of his daughter who had died from scarlet fever. The Crittenton movement flourished across the country

From 1976 to 2006, the foundation (known then as the National Florence Crittenton Mission) operated under the auspices of the Child Welfare League of America. In 2006, the decision was made to re-energize the foundation's work with the Crittenton family of agencies across the country. As a result, in 2007, the foundation opened its own headquarters in Portland, Oregon, in 2007. The foundation continues to support Crittenton agencies in their work to provide opportunities for vulnerable girls, young women, and their families to live healthy, safe, and self-sufficient lives.

Jeannette Pai-Espinosa took over as President in 2007. Throughout her career, Pai-Espinosa has been a vocal advocate and activist for issues of importance to girls and women. She is also an acknowledged expert on developing strategies to help individuals, organizations, and communities positively address ethnic and racial diversity.

No one is useless in this world who lightens the burden of it for someone else.

—BENJAMIN FRANKLIN

Charles Crittenton realized that most institutions of his day served men, and that if he really wanted to make a difference he would need to invest in the life of women. He created not only institutions, but a movement across the country and overseas to support women who wanted to turn their lives around. His views, and those of his co-Founder, Dr. Kate Waller Barrett, remain relevant today, especially the idea of addressing social problems through local communities.

What our foundation does is to invest in the power of potential. We focus on breaking inter-generational cycles of destructive behaviors and relationships and the stories of the young women who come through our doors is inspirational. A sixty-eight-year-old woman born in the Crittenton home outside Savannah, Georgia, was eventually adopted by a Crittenton board member. When she grew up and married, she became the Executive Director of the Crittenton agency in Charleston, South Carolina. Today, she continues to give back not just to that agency, but to our movement.

A woman who had been abused as a child now in her late thirties spent time at the Crittenton agency in a Fullerton, California, home when she was a young single mother—she and her young son were homeless and with nowhere to go. There she not only worked on her parenting skills but participated in therapeutic programs, education, and workforce training. She landed an internship with a company that eventually hired her. Today, she manages multi-million-dollar accounts for this business, and her son has just started college. Talk about breaking destructive cycles! I often talk to women who are looking for a way to give back in appreciation for the support they received. That's so inspiring!

Giving is about connecting to core values. Every individual does what she or he does because of the values that matter to them. To the extent that we can connect an organization or an issue with our core values determines the extent to which we will give. I personally come from a long line of activists. My grandfather was active in leading the revolutionary Democratic movement in Korea against Japanese occupation. My great grandfather had been executed in prison for the same cause. My mother worked for Planned Parenthood and supported the Equal Rights Amendment in the 1970s. In many ways, she combined traditional Korean values with a very American viewpoint. My father has always been an advocate for racial justice.

Many people believe that their giving is separate from what they do every day. I remember a woman who worked in retail but always had a passion for helping pregnant teens. She didn't think there was a way to combine her job with her passion, but we gave her some ideas and she ended up teaching them how to present themselves for jobs in a very professional manner.

MAKE A DIFFERENCE TODAY

People think of Bill Gates when they think about giving. But the nonprofit sector depends on small gifts they can count on year after year. The large, occasional donations are wonderful, but it's the ongoing contributions that make a difference by helping nonprofits stabilize and sustain themselves. It permits them to count on the future instead of worrying about if they will have funding tomorrow. Find a personal connection with the mission of an organization you choose to support. So feel good about the $25 or $50 check that you write every month—it really adds up.

VOLUNTEERING IS A HIGH

Janet Sharma, Executive Director,
Volunteer Center of Bergen County, Inc.

BergenVolunteers.org

On any given day in Bergen County, New Jersey, hundreds of people go to work assisting children, the elderly, the hungry, and the homeless. But they take home no paycheck, and they all share the same title, volunteer. They are part of a small army of givers affiliated with the Volunteer Center of Bergen County. They offer skills and companionship, share struggles, and help lessen the burdens faced by others in their community. The center is a member of the Points of Light Foundation and Hands On Network, a nonprofit, nonpartisan, national organization that works in partnership with approximately 350 volunteer connection groups nationwide to mobilize people to take action that can change the world. As well, the center is affiliated with the USA Freedom Corps sponsored by the White House, the Corporation for National and Community Service, and the Network for Good.

Janet Sharma is Executive Director of the center. The daughter of a community activist, Sharma got the message early in life that sitting around without lending a hand just isn't an option!

Remember that when you leave this earth, you can take
with you nothing that you have received—only what you

have given: a full heart, enriched by honest service, love, sacrifice, and courage.

—St. Francis of Assisi

The way people grow up—and around whom they grow up—has a huge influence on how they choose to live. For some people it's all about clothing and cars and trips and a kind of self-absorption. Then there are people who sense that what happens to the human race happens to them. A flood or earthquake or outbreak half a world away isn't a remote event. They connect with the people affected; it's just part of their giving spirit.

Volunteering gives people such a high! I like to tell a story about my own son, David, who grew up very close to Mario, a retired neighbor. Mario spent a lot of time with my son, teaching him how to mow the lawn and do other things around the house. When David was about six years old, Mario had a heart attack, and David wanted to do something for him. So he drew a picture of a drum set and brought it to Mario who loved the picture and the gesture. When he saw his friend's reaction David's eyes teared up, and he told us, "My heart is so full." *Do good—feel good* is my personal motto and that our center has adopted. Volunteering helps you feel so much more connected to the rest of the world. We all wake up under the same sun and go to sleep under the same moon. It's not that I'm my brother's keeper, but neither can I turn a blind eye. Giving is a mindset.

Our center was founded in 1966 to connect people with the opportunity to volunteer, and that's basically what we do today, although we've branched out considerably, including to businesses that want to get involved. One of our offerings is a mentoring program—at any given time we have about two hundred mentors helping kids, overwhelmed mothers, and others who need guidance. We also run a chore service in which volunteers conduct home repairs for the elderly and disabled. Every year we participate in National Family Volunteer Week, a way to kick off the holiday season of giving and service by making volunteering a family tradition.

Make a Difference Today

Share your wisdom and experience through mentoring. Mentoring benefits people at all ages and stages; it takes place one-on-one at schools, workplaces, and community centers. Don't underestimate the knowledge and skills you have to share. Others are eager to know what you've already learned. If *you* are in need of help, consider asking someone you admire to mentor you. Ask and you just might receive!

PASSIONATE PURSUITS
Melanie Sabelhaus, Entrepreneur and Philanthropist

Melanie Sabelhaus had a good idea for a business. She pursued it with her typical drive and energy, and the enterprise that resulted was taken public in 1997. But commercial success wasn't enough for Melanie, a human dynamo who discovered her true passion when she entered the world of women's philanthropy. Melanie began her professional career with IBM, where she moved into senior management before leaving to create a company that provided short-term, quality housing for executives on the move. As a philanthropist and volunteer, she raised millions and inspired thousands as Dational Chair of United Way's Tocqueville Women's Leadership Council and introduced the Tiffany Circle, the women's philanthropic arm of the American Red Cross. She is currently a partner in Superior Financial Group, where she makes micro loans to deserving entrepreneurs. Melanie remains a passionate and committed philanthropist.

> *I don't know what your destiny will be, but one thing I know: the only ones among you who will be really happy are those who have sought and found how to serve.*

> —ALBERT SCHWEITZER

"Find a way to give of your time, talent and treasure," my dad always said. He was a steelworker in Cleveland, and we certainly didn't have money, but we had a lot of love. My parents believed it was an essential part of life to be engaged in your community. After I took my company public, I remembered those words. Finally, I found myself with time, talent, and treasure to share. Around that time my husband, Bob, came home from a United Way meeting and said, "Melanie, there's a women's philanthropy movement going on—women giving in their own names, writing their own checks." Inspired by the incredible Bonnie McElveen-Hunter, founder of Pace Communications and first woman Chair of the American Red Cross, I got involved. We helped this revolution in women's philanthropy reach new heights through United Way's Tocqueville Women's Leadership, where we raised more than $100 million. Finally, we were chicks writing checks in our own names!

Women represent the fastest growing segment of the economy. Women start most businesses in this country, and they purchase 85 percent of all goods and services sold. And with women living an average of seven years longer than men and trillions of dollars transferring to them, women are the clearly most powerful voice in philanthropy today. I met an older woman in Oklahoma who had been dutifully writing her annual check to the American Red Cross for $200. When she handed us a check for $100,000 I asked her what had changed, and she answered, "It's simple. Nobody ever asked me before." These are the kinds of people who inspire me to make a big, bold difference.

MAKE A DIFFERENCE TODAY

People will support what they help create. A key to success in philanthropy is discovering what matters to your donor—find out where his or her passion lies and deliver on that. Put a face on your charity. Bring in a recipient of the money you're raising, and let that person tell donors why it matters. Let them feel it and touch it. It may bring tears to their eyes, but it will also bring understanding.

The Philosophy of Abundance
Sandra Yancey, Founder and CEO, eWomen Network

eWomenNetwork.com
eWomenFoundation.org

Sandra Yancey is proving for thousands of women what she long ago proved to herself—the best way to succeed is to collaborate. In 2000, she and her husband, Kym, created eWomenNetwork, an extensive network of female business owners and professionals. Their access to one another's skills, talents, knowledge, and connections is a unique resource and is the essence of the organization's success. At Accelerated Networking™ events across the United States and Canada, businesswomen build relationships and conduct business in an innovative, collaborative way.

An award-winning entrepreneur, author, broadcast personality, and philanthropist, Yancey created the eWomenNetwork Foundation to support the financial and emotional health of women and children, especially those most in need. The foundation has awarded hundreds of thousands of dollars in cash and donations to nonprofit organizations and to promising young female entrepreneurs. Yancey has been widely recognized for her creativity and ability to inspire.

As I give, I get.

—Mary McLeod Bethune

My five favorite words are, "How can I help you?" The most important thing I know about business success is that you can't make it on your own. At eWomenNetwork, we believe that by giving and being "other focused," you create a world of abundance for all. "If you want a friend, be a friend," my mother always said. If you want love, give love. And if you want success, give success. When it comes down to it, giving is the most renewable resource on the planet. As we give to one another, we are constantly renewed by what we've done, and those we help will grow and prosper, thus perpetuating the cycle to continue.

Whether it's in business or personal life, I believe you really haven't given until you've given to someone who can never pay you back. That's why when participants at our networking events share their business card with a handwritten lead on the reverse side, it's not a hollow gesture. It means you're giving someone access to you, and that you commit to give freely of yourself to someone who calls upon you. We call it the philosophy of abundance, and it really does create a glow in those who practice it.

Although I had no money with which to fund it, I started the foundation at the same time I started eWomenNetwork. I'll never forget the look of surprise on the face of the banker when I asked to open up a foundation account. "You can't actually do this," the banker told me. "You need an IRS 501(c)(3) designation." While waiting to get the correct paperwork processed, I opened up a charity account. I did this because I knew it only made sense to me to create a business if it would also be involved in charitable giving.

To no surprise, the more we gave, the more we were rewarded.

Following Hurricane Katrina, the foundation networked with Nike and the Women's NBA to adopt a girls' high school basketball team from Pass Christian, Mississippi, a hard-hit town that got very little media attention. When we arrived, the spirited members of the team were practicing in a steaming hot gym without air-conditioning, and several were without sneakers! We were able to provide them with all new basketball gear—including shoes, balls, uniforms, and other equipment; to see the joy and appreciation on their young faces was something I will never forget. CNN filmed the story and included the foundation in their American Hero series. We impacted these deserving girls not just by providing them with material things but by also exposing some of them to our International Conference later that summer, that provided them access and connections to Donna Orender, President of the WNBA, as well as several Hall of Fame female basketball players.

Make a Difference Today

Give what you want most and watch what comes back to you. When you give, you plant seeds that will grow for years to come. Find a way to provide others with access to their dreams, and do it without judgment about their choices or their vision. Help others achieve their dream, and give thanks to those who help you achieve yours. You will succeed in ways and to degrees you never imagined!

eXtra Special Caring
Gail Heyman, Board Member and Advocate,
The National Fragile X Foundation

FragileX.org

There is much to learn from people who live with and overcome intellectual disabilities, a category that includes autism, Down syndrome, fragile X syndrome, cerebral palsy, among other conditions. Gail Heyman, the mother of Scott Heyman, a young man with fragile X, is one of millions who are striving to make a difference as they raise a child with special needs. Serving on the Board of the National Fragile X Foundation and co-founder and President of The Fragile X Association of Georgia, Heyman knows the challenges first hand. Fragile X is a genetic disorder and the leading cause of inherited intellectual disabilities. The Heyman family chose to see Scott's diagnosis not as a disability but as a challenge for their son, their family, and disability advocates. Following the lessons of her parents, Scott's little sister, Carly, wrote the book *My eXtra Special Brother, How to Love, Understand and Celebrate Your Sibling with Special Needs* (available both in English and Spanish) and conducts sibling workshops nationwide.

The National Fragile X Foundation supports families by providing informational, referral, and emotional support, promoting awareness, developing educational materials and conferences, and supporting research for better treatments and an ultimate cure. Gail gives as she lives—wholly and with hope and joy.

When you teach your son, you teach your son's son.

—FROM THE TALMUD

Other than giving unconditional love, there is nothing more important than to be an encouraging voice for a child with special needs. As parents, we know that our child will need our positive voice to help him participate in the full spectrum of his life. We want to positively impact his success as a productive human being. We want to empower him to reach his potential and create an environment for him to be successful in his life. With the help of others in the community, we dream of the time that he creates his own self-determination and lives an independent life with our support. Together with family, friends, businesses, and nonprofits, we can move toward creating a better place in this world for individuals with special needs.

By opening up doors and welcoming people with disabilities, you are creating a more humane and understanding world. Even though we want self-reliance for our child, there must be a greater reliance on the businesses community and the community at large to offer accommodations in both school and work. In return, everyone benefits. I believe that people have a core need and desire to make an impact on the lives of others. That need gets filled when you help someone who is limited in his or her ability to be independent. What the giver gets back in return is bigger than the give. It is not a small thing to help others in need.

As an advocate, I have witnessed the joy of helping other families and have also been the beneficiary of services that I have advocated for. There are two sides of the coin with giving, and both matter greatly. There is one thing I know for sure: A benefactor never knows when they might become a beneficiary of compassionate services.

Make a Difference Today

If you own a business, assess the possibility of offering employment to an individual with special needs. If you are an individual, investigate becoming a pal or big brother or big sister to someone with special needs. Become a buddy and play on a Little League Challenger baseball team. Volunteer with the Special Olympics. Show your love and understanding to the sibling of a brother or sister with special needs. Don't underestimate the importance of lending a helping hand and showing your support to individuals with intellectual disabilities. You stand to get a lot more than you give.

CHAPTER 8

Giving Around the World

In writing this book, we found thousands and thousands of causes so great and so important we could write forever about them. It was overwhelming to learn of the endless needs there are and inspiring to see how these calls to action were being answered.

While we may never see the faces of the individuals that are the beneficiaries of the many challenges that plague our world and humankind, when we give to corners of the earth we will never see who need help, we rise to the greatest height of giving.

The organizations and individuals who are making a difference around the world receive our universal applause. They have gone beyond the boundaries of giving and found ways to volunteer or give their dollars, selecting a slice of the world and making a difference.

You, too, can reach out to those countries and communities who need a voice of concern and support, our time, and our dollars. Select a global cause, and then focus on your time and take action. Participate in a known global cause, or give time in a place or cause where few if any have ever gone before. Search the ends of the earth and back for a way to make others' lives and their missions count.

GIVING VOICE

Melanne Verveer, Founder, Chair, and Co-CEO,
The Vital Voices Global Partnership

VitalVoices.org

The Vital Voices Global Partnership is a non-governmental organization (NGO) that identifies, trains, and empowers women leaders and social entrepreneurs around the world. Vital Voices believes in the transformative value of women's participation in society. Its investment in women creates economic opportunities, advances political reform, and safeguards human rights. Through its leadership development and local empowerment programs, Vital Voices works to expand women's influential roles around the world. Melanne Verveer is Founder and current Co-CEO. Vital Voices Global Leadership network now reaches over five thousand women in eighty-five countries.

What a joy to witness women around the globe using their voices as leaders.

—MELANNE VERVEER

Service is critically important to a satisfying life. A quote often attributed to Martin Luther King, Jr., tells us that service is the rent we pay for occupying the space we take up on earth. Inspired from an early age, Melanne felt a strong calling to public service. The potential impact can be so great when one can influence an outcome, just like the civil rights movement or any other worthy cause. But public service also offers a personal reward where one learns the important lessons of life, transmitted and transferred to each generation.

Having done my graduate work in Russian studies and with the end of the Cold War, I was excited about the prospect of working with women who were making the transition from living under communism to building a democratic society. The women from Eastern Europe, Russia, and Ukraine were going through tough times. If the new market economies were going to prosper and nascent democracies were to flourish, women had to become effective leaders. Through Vital Voices we helped them build skills in key areas, from communications and advocacy to growing a business. We were able to help them make a difference.

The impact of serving others has been instrumental for the betterment of society. Vital Voices provides women with the capacity, connections, and credibility they need to unlock their leadership potential. At the forefront of international coalitions to combat human trafficking and all forms of violence against women and girls, Vital Voices stands to make the world a better place.

Vital Voices originated from the United States government's successful Vital Voice Democracy Initiative. During the United Nations Fourth World Conference on Women in Beijing in 1995, over 180 country representatives supported the advancement of women. The United States made a series of commitments to further women's progress at home and globally. Since its inception,

Vital Voices has provided skills, networking opportunities, and the ability and link to support women around the world.

No matter how different women are, no matter where they live, they have far more in common than their differences. They want to participate in their societies and give back to their communities. Society is finally recognizing that the investments in women will improve the world. The World Bank, the World Economic Forum, and other influential institutions have compiled empirical data that shows a direct correlation between investments in women and alleviation of poverty and a country's overall prosperity.

Once the Vital Voices Democracy Initiative was established, women began to build a new movement of leaders into the world. These women are now taking their advocacy, communication, and policy skills to other women. These new professional networks are establishing a great collaborative partnership for women globally.

Today, the Vital Voices Global Partnership enables women to become change agents in their governments, to advocate for social justice, and to support democracy and the rule of law. Additionally, when women learn better management, business development, marketing, and communications skills to expand their enterprises, they not only provide for their families but create jobs in their communities.

There is also a growing belief that women can access levels of power in all sectors of society. Vital Voices' work has always been with women whose leadership creates better societies. The women pay the investment made in them forward. They go on to make significant contributions to enhance the public good. When an investment is made in one woman through training and mentoring, she will go on and train others. The investment grows exponentially. Essentially, training the trainers can be very challenging, but the payoffs will be tremendous.

MAKE A DIFFERENCE TODAY

Consider using the leadership skills you've perfected at work to enhance your giving. Your ability to make things happen might translate into starting a chapter of a nonprofit that you admire. Or it might mean hosting a speaker at your home to introduce a cause or movement in your community. Giving leadership can be extremely rewarding.

WORKING TOWARD A GREENER, CLEANER WORLD

Kim McKay, Co-Founder and Deputy Chairwoman, Clean Up the World

cleanuptheworld.org

Clean Up the World is among the largest green initiatives on the planet, with 35 million volunteers worldwide. It has its roots in Australia in 1987 when yachtsman Ian Kiernan was sailing solo around the world. He was shocked to see so much pollution in and around some of the world's most beautiful waterways. Inspired by his concern, Kim McKay, a PR Executive, joined Kiernan in organizing a one-day effort to clean up Sydney Harbor in January, 1989. Their longing for a cleaner, greener world hit a nerve—forty thousand people turned out, and together they pulled some five thousand tons of trash out of the harbor. Kiernan and McKay dedicated themselves to replicating these efforts in other Australian cities. They wrote a manual and produced a video about how to organize community cleanups, and requests for it came in from around the world.

Today, Clean Up the World does more than remove trash. The organization is active in 120 countries. In partnership with the United Nations Environment Programme (UNEP), it advocates for new water technology, lobbies lawmakers, and raises funds in Australia for pollution control. In June, 2008, McKay was honored for two decades of environmental advocacy and community service when she received an Order of Australia (AO), one of the country's highest citizen awards. She is the co-author of the *True Green* series of books on protecting the environment.

> *We do not inherit the earth from our ancestors; we borrow it from our children.*

> —NATIVE AMERICAN PROVERB

I've been on what I call a long and accidental green journey. Since I was a child I've been interested in community service and volunteering. I come from a middle class family where there was never much spare cash, but I realized that I could give my time to help people even if I couldn't give money. We all know the importance of awareness, but the actual act of doing something is incredibly powerful in changing behavior.

One of my favorite stories is about a project we did with some of the indigenous communities in Western Australia's Kimberley region. We were cleaning up a huge stretch of desert at the request of the Aboriginal leaders. But what was so important was that the project was done their way, with culturally consistent materials designed by indigenous artists. The work is never just about the environment—it's always about the community and the individuals involved. We've come so far—one of our newest projects is a partnership with Google that is helping us build a global platform to register and map worldwide community cleanups online.

We designed Clean Up the World as a free and open resource for people to use as they wish. We offer them our logo and our experience and networks and ask them to sign a simple letter stating that they will abide by certain standards. This decentralized approach works, because our goal is not to control people and what they do but to empower them. When you do that, you can move mountains. And in our case, we move mountains of rubbish!

Make a Difference Today

Small things really do make a difference in creating a greener, cleaner world. Start by taking a look at your personal energy consumption. Turn off and unplug appliances that aren't being used. Consider walking or biking to work if possible. Look for hands-on ways to help, like clean-up events in your community. If you can't find one, consider starting one by going to the website for more information. Imagine the collective impact of reducing our carbon emissions if we all did these things.

An Inspired Life

Tom Gittins, Chair of Gittins & Associates;
Sister Cities and the Peace Corps

www.sister-cities.org

www.peacecorps.gov

Inspired by President John F. Kennedy's urging to "Ask not what your country can do for you, ask what you can do for your country," Tom Gittins left his insurance business and joined the Peace Corps at age twenty-seven as Associate Director in the Dominican Republic. His experience left an indelible imprint. It inspired his life's work—connecting Americans with faraway people and places. When he left as Director of the Peace Corps in the Dominican Republic, he became Chief of Operations for the Latin American Region of the Peace Corps in Washington. In 1971, he assumed leadership of Sister Cities International, which he helped grow from a handful of cities engaged in international educational, cultural, and professional exchange to thousands. In 1992, he launched Gittins & Associates, a consulting services firm specializing in international programs and projects and inspired by his Peace Corps service. Gittins is active on the board of a foundation created by fellow Peace Corps volunteers and staff that raises money for scholarships for low-income Dominicans. He was a founding board member of the International Exchange Association, a consortium of citizen exchange organizations. He has served on the boards of a number of international training, education, and exchange organizations. A man making an ongoing difference, he shares his lessons of giving.

We travel, some of us forever, to seek other states, other lives, other souls.

—ANAIS NIN

Through my consulting business helping people connect globally with causes, I've had the privilege of working with foundations adopting Russian children and groups of plastic surgeons who travel across the world to repair the cleft palates of children born with birth defects. There's a wealth of desire and capability out there—people really want to reach out and give. But you don't have to go far away to touch people across the world. Any time anyone goes beyond their own borders, whatever the reason, it opens up a whole new world. The Roanoke, Virginia, school system filled a trunk with American artifacts and sent it to their Korean sister city to familiarize them with the lives of Americans. Their Korean counterparts did the same. That simple gesture promoted understanding and acceptance across tens of thousands of miles.

Around the time I was starting my own business, I read a speech by Ralph Lazarus that really moved me. At the time he was Chairman of Federated Department Stores. Lazarus was predicting the future of volunteerism, and he observed that as people live longer and longer, and as technology advances, we're going to see individuals with much more time on their hands to volunteer. His words inspired me to do everything I could to help encourage global outreach and volunteering.

I see an extraordinary level of capability and desire on the part of the American public to get involved—to do something! That can take the shape of anything from a school child hooking up with a pen pal, to a city manager helping to train foreign colleagues, or a cultural exchange between politically unfriendly nations. A new endeavor in which I'm involved is the U.S. Center for Citizen Diplomacy, dedicated to dramatically increasing the number of Americans engaged as private citizens or citizen diplomats.

One of the many benefits of volunteerism is personal fulfillment and self-satisfaction—I don't know many Peace Corps volunteers who say that they gave more out of the experience than they got. I think it's absolutely okay to feel that you're getting skills and experience that will help you in your professional life. You see this spirit among professional volunteers—city managers, health directors, water specialists, and other municipal officials are traveling across the globe to share what they know with counterparts in other countries. They're doing it because they care and because they gain a great deal of personal satisfaction. There are so many ways to change lives for the better—it doesn't always take a lot of money; but it does take commitment and effort.

Make a Difference Today

When you choose a way to reach out, make sure it's connected to something you love, whether it's other countries, the environment, or the arts. Enjoy the work, and feel good about gaining skills that will help you in other aspects of your life. Don't hesitate to list on your résumé experiences and capabilities that you've gained in the nonprofit world.

The Gift of Sleeping in Safety
Kathy Bushkin Calvin, Executive Vice President and Chief Operating Officer, The United Nations Foundation

UNFoundation.org

Kathy Bushkin Calvin is Executive Vice President and Chief Operating Officer of the United Nations Foundation, which was created in 1998 with an historic gift from philanthropist and businessman Ted Turner. The foundation builds partnerships to address poverty, disease, the environment, and other pressing world problems. Following a career in politics and communications, Calvin led AOL Time Warner's philanthropic activities. She is a member of several nonprofit boards, including Share Our Strength and City Year.

I feel the capacity to care is the thing which gives life its deepest significance.

—Pablo Casals

Every thirty seconds, a child dies of malaria in Africa. Through our "Nothing But Nets" campaign, anyone can donate a $10 bed net to protect children from being bitten by a malaria-carrying mosquito. I visited a UN bed net distribution center in Senegal, and it was so exciting to see Africans taking ownership of their own families' health. You could see the pride on the part of mothers who were so grateful to be *doing something*. It's so empowering. And that's what we try to do at the UN Foundation—empower those who give *and* those who receive.

There are two categories of givers as I see it. One group wants to be unique and have their names associated with their good works, and that's wonderful. The other group wants to partner with something that's already working to make an impact. That's the group we appeal to. Our challenge is to give those who want to contribute globally the comfort that their money is going to effective programs that are monitored and measured. And that's the case whether it's a $10 bed net or a $10,000 clinic.

Just in the area of malaria prevention, there have been so many positive developments. Recent changes mean bed nets no longer have to be re-dipped in insecticide every year. The new nets last about five years, and the $10 covers the purchase and distribution as well as educating the family about how to use it. In one village, I watched the kids put on a wonderful skit explaining why the bed nets work and keep them alive. It was incredibly powerful.

Now families in need are getting even more out of the bed nets. That's because when they come to the local medical tents that serve as distribution centers, the foundation is also providing childhood vaccinations and essential vitamin A pills. It comes down to this: Our donors are saving children's lives by allowing them to sleep safely at night.

MAKE A DIFFERENCE TODAY

Many companies today are trying to figure out how they can help encourage people's desire to give. If you work where employee volunteerism is encouraged, that's great. If you don't, demand it! Check out sites like FreeRice.com and Avaaz.org. They give you a tremendous opportunity to feel like giving is part of who you are and what you do every day.

Improving Global Ties One Handshake at a Time

Ann Olsen Schodde, Executive Director, U.S. Center for Citizen Diplomacy

USCenterforCitizenDiplomacy.org

The U.S. Center for Citizen Diplomacy promotes the involvement of Americans in foreign relations. The idea, says Executive Director Ann Schodde, is that you do not have to be a member of the diplomatic corps serving overseas to influence the perception of the United States abroad. In fact, she says, although we may not think of ourselves as citizen diplomats, we are every time we interact with those from foreign countries in school, at work, and in social settings. The center believes volunteerism is the best way to encourage citizen diplomacy and promotes participation through its national data base of international volunteer opportunities, education and training programs, and national recognition of U.S. citizens who have made outstanding contributions as citizen diplomats. Schodde has been involved in international relations and education for her entire thirty-year career. She has consulted with and held leadership positions in organizations including the Carnegie Council on Ethics and International Affairs, Sister Cities International, U.S. Ukraine Foundation, National University for Continuing Education Association, and National Council of International Visitors. She has testified before Congress on the importance of federal support for international education and exchange programs.

> *"Never doubt that a small group of thoughtful, committed*
> *citizens can change the world; indeed, it is the only thing*
> *that ever has."*

—MARGARET MEAD

There is a massive movement of people from all over the world relocating from one place to another. Past generations of Americans could get by with relatively little understanding of other cultures, but that is no longer the case. Today, frequently we interact with people from other countries in every facet of our lives. At the center, we believe volunteering is the best way to promote citizen diplomacy. It can be something as simple as helping your child exchange letters or emails with a friend from another country or assisting new immigrants in your community learn English. When we develop these relationships, we no longer think of them as someone from another country, we think about them as a friend, even when their country of origin might be one in which the United States is engaged in conflict. As citizens of one of the richest and most powerful nations in the world, it is not only a right but a responsibility of all Americans to find ways to participate on the world stage and to do so with understanding and respect for cultures other than our own. It does not always have to involve traveling abroad. Every time we interface with someone from another country, we are representing the values and principles upon which this country was founded. That is what it means to be a citizen diplomat.

Consider Anjali Bhatia, a college student who was one of our 2008 national scholarship winners. In Kolkata, she worked with the Bengal Rural Welfare Services to empower women in rural villages through micro-loans. She also spent time living and working in Rwanda, where new friends told stories about living as refugees and watching family members murdered. This type of outreach builds bridges across continents, one citizen at a time. On the other hand, a third-grade teacher, Khris Nedam, in Michigan has worked every year with her students to raise money for Kids4AfghanKids. Their efforts, without leaving the classroom, have built schools and an orphanage in Afghanistan.

I was blessed with wonderful parents. Although they did not have a lot of money and they were not able to travel abroad or send me on foreign exchange programs, they taught me a valuable lesson that has great relevance to my work. The always reminded me that my "home is the center, but it should never be the boundary," always encouraging me to seek out new friendships and experiences.

MAKE A DIFFERENCE TODAY

Committing to three years in the Peace Corps is an important commitment, but it is just one way to get involved as a citizen diplomat. You can invite a foreign student studying at a nearby university to your home for dinner or a holiday. Get involved in the Sister Cities or IV programs, or work with your children's schools to ensure that foreign languages and cultures are being introduced as early as possible.

CREATING INSTITUTIONS THAT WILL BECOME PILLARS OF DEMOCRACY
Sarah Carey, Chair, Eurasia Foundation

Eurasia.org

Sarah Carey, a partner in the law firm Squire, Sanders & Dempsey LLP, is the longtime volunteer Chairwoman of the Eurasia Foundation. She discovered years ago a way to combine her professional interests and personal passions. The result is an enormous contribution to enriching life in former Soviet countries. Eurasia Foundation is a nonprofit that receives support from the United States Agency for International Development and other donors. Since 1992, the foundation has invested more than $360 million in programs in Russia, Ukraine, the countries of Central Asia and of the Caucasus, and other nations. The group's work is different from that of other nonprofits—rather than provide needed goods and services to individuals, Eurasia Foundation establishes and teaches local people to operate democratic institutions like schools, local government agencies, and social service agencies. It also supports the creation of smaller businesses and local independent newspapers that help nurture the emerging middle class.

The more I help others to succeed, the more I succeed.

—RAY KROC

In college I majored in Russian history and did graduate work in the former Soviet Union. After law school I worked for a public interest law firm and always kept a hand in civil rights and social problems, including those in Russia, even after my career focused on corporate law. So I was very excited to be invited in the late 1980s to join a delegation to meet with former Premier Gorbachev, who told us his country was ready for a role on the global economic stage. I was inspired to begin building a legal practice representing companies investing in the region. Since I was spending so much of my professional time focused on these countries, I decided I should dedicate my volunteer time as well.

The Eurasia Fund was new in 1992, and it was appealing because it responded to *local* needs like establishing independent presses, schools, and research centers—what I call civic institutions. Because everything in the former Soviet countries was state run, citizens had never taken responsibility for their own communities and responsibilities. But that's changed, and now citizens are developing local economic plans, taking steps to make sure immigrants are treated fairly, and taking responsibility for their own communities. The foundation is showing people how to play a role in improving local education, social services, and even tax collections. The business schools we support are also having an impact. Training students to be first rate, ethical business leaders, they'll be able to run companies that will some day list on the London stock exchange while at the same time boosting their own local economies.

These are the kinds of institutions, we believe, that will become pillars of democracy in the former Soviet countries. What's encouraging is that other funders have been attracted as a result of the seed funding Eurasia Foundation has provided. Most exciting is what's happening in the countries themselves, where local philanthropists are getting involved in establishing and supporting their own democratic institutions.

We are also working to create legacy institutions in the regions where we have a mandate. This is being done by spinning off locally managed regional foundations that will pursue the goals that have driven Eurasia Foundation for fifteen years.

Make a Difference Today

Consider becoming a volunteer in an area related to your profession or personal interests. Whether you're a lawyer, teacher, student, stay-at-home parent, or retired, choose something that connects with your abilities and passions. When you align with a cause that has a deep, personal connection, the cause takes root in your heart and becomes part of who you are.

A MATTER OF THE HEART
Sung-Joo Kim, Founder and CEO, Sungjoo Group,
MCM Products AG

One of the most celebrated businesswomen in Asia, Sung-Joo Kim is equally well known for her life-changing philanthropy, especially her support of humanitarian efforts in North Korea. She is a Founder of Sungjoo Group and is Chairperson of MCM Group/MCM Products Ag./MCM Lederwarn GmbH. The group has successfully launched globally renowned brands and retail operations including Gucci, Yves Saint Laurent, Sonia Rykiel, and Marks & Spencer. The company has also acquired MCM's global business, distributing to more than 150 retailers in forty countries, and the estimated revenue in 2008 is more than 200MUSD. She is the author of the best-selling collection of autobiographical essays, *Wake-up Call—A Beautiful Outcast*. She has earned global recognition for her business and philanthropic achievements.

> *Real generosity toward the future lies in giving all to the present.*

> —ALBERT CAMUS

My upbringing was an interesting combination of traditional Confucianism on my father's side plus puritanical Christianity on my mother's side. So I was raised in a very strict living style

that meant no earthly pleasures and male superiority. I was forced
to accept an arranged marriage with an appropriate partner. But
when I rebelled, I was thrown out of the family. I made my way to
New York, where I got my start in the fashion industry working at
Bloomingdale's. Although it was very unusual for a young Korean
woman with my upbringing and education to be working in a
department store, I learned retailing first hand which was a step to
helping me build my own fashion empire.

The more I got into the work, the more I was drawn to social
justice issues. My father was always a very honest businessman
and, despite our differences, I emulated him in that way. In a
country known for bribery and corruption, he remained apolitical.
And although I had separated myself from my family, I continued
to be influenced by him and by my mother who carried herself
so humbly. She used only a small percentage of the household
money she received from my father and gave the rest to charity.
My father questioned why she did not buy diamonds and crystal
glasses like other wealthy women, and I always complained, too,
wondering why families humbler than ours seemed to have
more. And although my lifestyle is very different from that of my
family, I find myself somewhat like my mother today, choosing
few extravagances for myself.

When my father passed away, my three brothers alone inherited
an empire worth billions, which motivated me even more to build
my own business. I also saw in the business world how the rich
get richer and the poor become poorer. I could not believe that

such a tiny percentage of businesses dominated the market and the economy, and I felt I had to do something about it. So my company returns 10 percent of its net profits, and I return 30-40 percent of my personal salary. We donate food and medicine in North Korea through several foundations and organizations. The people there, including some distance family of mine, are basically starving to death, and at least 3 million are impacted by TB due to poor nutrition and lack of vaccines.

Regarding women's economic empowerment, I feel very good to have helped mobilize some of the major IT companies in the world, including Microsoft, IBM, and Samsung. I've helped them see that Intelligence Quotient (IQ) plus emotional quotient (EQ) equals WQ, or women's quality. What that means in a twenty-first century economy is letting women compete as knowledge-based workers to learn and earn! I challenge companies to develop their corporate social responsibility. I tell them that women are their primary customers who care for ethical and fair trading, and they are the most revolutionary vehicle to correct their societies and to grow the future economy around the globe. Sure, it's a money matter, but it's really a matter of the heart.

My company has also been involved in setting up a school in Calcutta and a hospital in Madagascar, and we've funded many women's economic summits. We recently established a Global Women's Leadership Center exchanging young women around the globe to learn cultural and leadership skills. Sure it's a money matter, but it's really a matter of the heart.

Make a Difference Today

Your enthusiasm and dedication can turn around the big guys and the big power, because when your heart is in your effort, you will be inspired to serve creatively, which will produce bigger outcomes. Find logical connections between givers you know. Connect someone building a school with someone involved in giving away books. There's tremendous synergy around giving, and you can be part of it.

CHAPTER 9

Technology with a Heart

CASEY GOLDEN, FOUNDER AND CEO, SMALL ACT NETWORK

In the land of philanthropy, technology has not only played a part, but it has completely revolutionized the entire landscape. Traditional giving—in the form of financial donations, as well as volunteering—has been escalated to entirely new levels, and it is now possible to give in ways that would have simply not existed without the technological advancements of the last decade. Today, giving takes literally *seconds*.

Online giving and volunteering from home are just two of the very simple, yet profound examples of what has been made possible. These examples of small acts philanthropy are ways that every person can participate, unlocking the huge potential of a mass collaborative effort. That one dollar you can give today, or the one hour you can volunteer, means so much because that small commitment can be shared by the other hundreds of millions of people in the United States—and by the billions globally. Smaller actions and requirements enable every single person to participate and truly be a meaningful, active part of the change they wish to see.

Another amazing advancement is in the category of interactive philanthropy. What is so special about this is that it opens the door for people to develop a much closer and longer term relationship with charities and causes they believe in. By donating more frequently with smaller gifts, donors are able to chart progress and see how well a charity is using a gift before committing larger sums of money. Seeing progress through website updates, emails, and blogs provides donors with a much better visibility, trust, and knowledge that their donation is truly having impact.

The last, but definitely not the least of the general categories is global awareness and action, which is now a powerful driving force in philanthropy. With the advent of the Internet, information can be accessed from anyone—anywhere in the world—and communication between people has blossomed with this newfound freedom. Going beyond the websites and emails prevalent in the '90s, social networks and other peer-to-peer communication vehicles—such as blogs and online videos—have completely changed the landscape. It is becoming virtually impossible to think of our lives without them! Social networking has increased both the speed and reach of important information—such as philanthropic successes, heartwarming journeys of passionate volunteers, and stories of those desperately in need of help—and provides the ability to unite like-minded people from around the world to work together to address important issues and find solutions.

The remainder of this chapter is dedicated to providing specific examples of how these advancements in technology have made a difference, and several ways you can immediately start giving and further your philanthropic goals.

QUICKLY AND EASILY BECOME A SAVVY DONOR

One of the most generally transformative effects of technology in philanthropy is in the availability of information. It is no longer a problem choosing a charity or learning about it, but it can be challenging to sort through the multitude of information that you obtain.

This is a good problem to have. There exist some amazing services and blogs that do 90 percent of the leg work for you—organizing the information into standardized formats for easy comparison and providing subjective insight beyond statistical analysis.

Charity Navigator

One of the most helpful services that gathers and sorts the data about nonprofits is called Charity Navigator (www.Charity Navigator.org). They do a fantastic job at organizing information, including crucial pieces of information such as financial details and how efficiently a charity is run. This is a truly outstanding resource that helps you choose the best charity for you.

In addition to statistical information, Charity Navigator provides a thorough Resources and Tips section that includes insightful information such as Top 10 Best Practices of Savvy Donors, What To Do When Charities Call, Tips for Giving in Times of Crisis, and many more.

It is always a very, very good idea to do your research before donating so you can make sure that your hard-earned money has the impact you seek. Charity Navigator makes this process as simple as can be.

Blogs

Blogs are fascinating new communication vehicles that have surfaced mostly in the last three years. A good way to describe a blog is as a personal diary that is posted publicly where factual information is presented but is infused with the personality, humor, passion, and the experiences of the writer.

Blogs are quickly becoming a popular means of disseminating information, similar to the feverish pace we saw in the late '90s when companies created their inaugural websites. Blogs are used across many different areas of business and entertainment, but the common thread linking them is that they are typically a person's (or persons) opinion on a particular matter.

Another captivating feature of blogs is that they are poised to be interactive, as readers are encouraged to comment on blog entries. This allows the readers to be a part of the discussion and to communicate their take on the topic to other interested readers. This makes for an excellent forum, as it enables readers to gain insight from many different angles—which they then use as a basis for their own well-rounded opinion.

In relation to giving and philanthropy, blogs have not yet been proven to directly increase donations, but they have certainly paved the way for significant social progress. By creating increased awareness and passion amongst readers, blogs create waves of supporters who become powerful currents that carry the boats of social progress to entirely new levels. They don't only help build a bigger boat (i.e., raise more money), but they help push that boat farther than it would have gone on its own.

There are also blogs focused on helping people looking to donate, who want more personal, experiential guidance. Following are several blogs put together by those seeking an even better way to choose the best charities with whom they want to become involved:

http://blog.givewell.net/

GiveWell believes that in giving, as in everything else, generosity and good intentions are nice, but not enough: Nonprofits should be thoroughly analyzed and compared against each other to determine which ones can most improve the world.

http://www.philanthromedia.org/
PhilanthroMedia was established for discerning donors who want to increase the impact of their giving.

http://charityandphilanthropy.blogspot.com/
This blog offers interviews with philanthropists about their foundations, trusts, and views; appeals and information on the general topic of giving; and service providers around the industry.

http://philanthropy.com/giveandtake/
The Chronicle has compiled this summary of blog postings of interest to people in the nonprofit world.

Spread the word ... and fast!

Undoubtedly, two of the most significant changes that technology has had on giving are the speed and reach of the "viral network" and the inspiration of online videos. The Internet, as well as its new services, has created an amazing opportunity for causes and passionate people to get immediate support from others around the world. The information spreads with such velocity because of how connected people are today (how many times a day do we check email?), and also because of the advancement of social networks. Because of this multi-layer connectivity, when new information hits the Web in the form of text or video, millions of people are instantly commenting on topics and sharing with others they know. While we have been familiar with the amazing speed of the Internet since the mid-nineties, these new advancements have raised the bar and created a whole new platform for communication and giving.

Social Networks

Facebook has become one of the most popular applications and sites of all time. One of the applications on this site, the "Causes" application has been available only for a little over a year, but has already made an amazing impact on giving. The creator of Causes, Napster co-creator Sean Parker, used his technology skills and insight to enable Facebook users to quickly communicate to their friends which issues and causes are important to them. This rapidly gathers support and brings more followers to the cause.

Breaking down how this happens, on Facebook, you first build a network of trusted friends with whom you want to share information. Whenever one of your friends changes any of their information (such as a favorite song, profile picture, or adding new people to their network), these changes appear as text on your home page. The result is that you have a virtual dashboard that shows you what is going on with all of your friends.

With respect to giving, this has created a simple platform on which charities can garner support from tens of thousands—if not millions—of people in a very short period of time. When one of your friends adds a charity to their Causes list (when your friend declares support for a specific charity), that notification appears on your own dashboard. Because they are a trusted friend to you, the statistics show that you are one hundred times more likely to look into (and consider supporting) that charity.

This creates an unbelievable acceleration of the already blazingly fast spread of information on the Internet. In addition to simply informing you of what is important to your friends, it provides easy access for you to take an action step where you can become a supporter of your friend's charity and easily contribute money to the cause.

The Causes application, which was released in November of 2006, noted that there are already 12.5 million people who have added the Causes on Facebook, and have used it to donate over $2.5 million in 2007. It is an amazing feat for such a new application to have this type of impact in its first year of use. So many causes have benefited from this newfound source of trusted giving, and the future looks even more dazzling.

Online Video

The world of online video has not only dramatically changed how many of us now access much of our entertainment, but has created a compelling and provocative way for people to express themselves, their passion, and their love. Because the communication boundaries of text and static pictures have been completely eliminated, people are now able to make videos and share them around the world for free—to anyone who wants to watch. Videos can range from sharing a baby's first steps with grandparents, to hilarious comedy skits, to amazing displays of talent, to incredible pet tricks, to political music videos, and also to heartfelt communication.

The hands-down leader of (and pioneer in) social online video is YouTube (www.youtube.com). Not only are people using words to gather support and communicate their thoughts, but with the advent of this service, the power of persuasion and inspiration has reached a new level. There are so many examples, but one amazing story that shows the groundbreaking impact is a simple video of a man giving free hugs that sparked a global Free Hug Day in a matter of months. For those who have not seen this video, it is a truly moving example of how someone, penniless, can have a transformative effect—and bring much-needed smiles to millions of people around the world. Following is the link to the video on YouTube. (http://www.youtube.com/watch?v=vr3x_RRJdd4).

This video is a remarkable example of how the definition of giving is expanding and changing in our digital world. Previously, giving money and volunteering your time were the most significant ways to help further a cause. Now, even those without extra money to give—or much time to share—can make a huge difference.

In no way is this intended to diminish the immense value of financial donations and volunteering; if anything, the hope is to increase both of those, but its most significant importance is to enhance and inspire others, no matter what you are giving. If you volunteer, use your camera phone to take a short video of your efforts or of the gracious people benefiting from your work. Nothing speaks more loudly than the faces of those being helped. If you feel compelled to write a poem about a cause, record a video of yourself reading the poem, post it to YouTube, and share the experience with potentially millions of people who might be moved into action. Using whatever skills with which you are blessed, online video is a simple (and free!) way to share your gift and give immediately. Do it. Share it. And inspire others.

GIVE WHAT YOU CAN. IT MEANS A LOT.

With the remarkable advancements in technology and the Internet, people are able to have a much more direct connection to the charities and causes that they care about. Technology has made philanthropy much easier and less time consuming, and more and more of us are becoming involved. Whether giving money, time, or support, the following organizations are just some of the amazing new offerings that help us give.

Volunteer Match—Connecting you with local volunteer opportunities

Volunteering has endless possibilities. The difficulty used to be looking through the phone book, searching online, or asking friends if they knew of any volunteer opportunities. Volunteer Match (www.VolunteerMatch.com) has addressed this need by providing an awesome site that connects you with volunteer opportunities perfect for you.

This is a phenomenal resource to find volunteer opportunities in your local area that need your help. They do a fantastic job in grouping volunteer activities into age groups and types of activities. This makes it tremendously easy to find exactly the right opportunity for you, your friends, or your kids.

Recently, they introduced two great services: Employee Volunteer Programs and Virtual Volunteer opportunities.

The Employee Volunteer Program is designed to help businesses of all sizes get into their communities and help out where it is needed most. The goal with this program is to help corporate social responsibility programs make the biggest impact that they can, both for the employees as well as the nonprofits. They describe this service as "Good Companies Helping Good Causes."

The Virtual Volunteer opportunities is an amazingly innovative program in which you can help your favorite organizations from wherever you are, at whatever time is convenient for you. Projects range from helping create PowerPoint presentations to being a volunteer coordinator to helping fill out accounting forms—and many, many more. The beauty of this is that it enables volunteers to use business skills to help organizations have huge impact, and volunteers can accomplish this from the comfort of home. This is an outstanding way to use technology to connect nonprofits to the virtual work force.

Whether you volunteer in person or virtually, VolunteerMatch is an exceptional resource. You don't have to waste time searching for a meaningful way to help; just spend your time doing it!

To get involved, simply go to www.VolunteerMatch.com.

DonorsChoose.org—Donating directly to your choice of projects

When Charles Best was teaching social studies at a school in Bronx, New York, he and his fellow teachers were commenting on how the lack of basic school supplies for students was having a detrimental effect, and was holding them back from being able to engage in a proper education. The teachers were contributing as much as they could afford to provide for the children (out of their own pockets), but it was not enough. They needed help from the people and businesses in the surrounding area who cared as much about these children's education as they did.

It was the beginning of something remarkable: Charles launched DonorsChoose.org. In this organization, they dramatically changed philanthropy by using technology to make a direct connection between the donors and the children who need them most. Teachers create projects at DonorsChoose.org for which they need additional supplies and funding, and donors go to the site and choose the specific project they want to support. This is a simple, brilliant way to have a project registry that enables donors to pick *exactly* what project (at which school) they feel is most important.

Not only do donors receive the gratification of real-time feedback, knowing that they have empowered local education, but also, donors have commented that the most rewarding part of the process is the letter and photos they receive back from the students whose project they funded. This simple, heartfelt thank you is priceless and lets donors know how much they have impacted the children's' lives

Another amazing use of this technology is how DonorsChoose. org is working with businesses such as Crate and Barrel, who give their customers a gift card to redeem at DonorsChoose.org to use it toward a project of their choosing. This has not only been a huge success for the kids, but also for the businesses, which have seen a significant increase in customer loyalty and purchasing because of their participation in this program.

With respect to technology, Charles Best says it well … *best*, when he said, "We simply could not exist without technology. By enabling real-time exchanges between a giver and recipient, this has by extension enabled a vast array of transparency and feedback. Technology has made it possible for ordinary folks to become philanthropists and get respect and accountability, no matter what the size of their donation."

To get involved, go to their website, www.DonorsChoose.org, and find the project that is perfect for you.

CaringBridge.org—Giving love and support when it's more precious than gold

When a close friend was hit with a tragic personal crisis, Sona Mehring was tasked to keep all of the friends and family in touch with what was going on. Knowing how overwhelming and time-consuming it would be to try to constantly update dozens of people by phone, Sona relied on her technology background to create something much more valuable than she ever imagined.

Her first step was to create a simple website for her friend, enabling her to post updates and messages and providing friends and family with one place from which to get the latest information. This dramatically saved time, but the most amazing part was yet to come.

Friends and family were also allowed to leave their own comments of love and support, which Sona's friend could read at a time that was convenient for her. Unbeknownst to Sona, this was the part of the technology that became the miracle worker. The abundant love, encouragement, and care that all of the friends and family were able to express literally became one of—if not the most important thing during this serious health condition.

Because of this experience, when Sona saw just how truly amazing and essential this service was at such an emotional and important time, she created CaringBridge.org so everyone would be able to easily create their own site (free) at critical times in life. The service is very simple and provides the necessary updates and communications for friends and family, but also helps with these three important areas while dealing with serious health issues:

1. It has been found that if the patients themselves feel that they are isolated and their hopes go down, there is a much higher risk of depression, long recovery times, and even mortality.

2. For the caregivers (spouse, children, etc.), they themselves are much more likely to fall ill because they

are overwhelmed and stressed, not only about the health issue, but with the pressure and burden of managing all the updates and communications.

3. As a friend or family member, it is so difficult to know when to help and when to give space. Too often, the love and support is abundant in the beginning, but then dramatically decreases after diagnosis because they do not want to interfere, say something awkward, or overwhelm their loved one. They do not know how exactly they can help, so they end up not helping at all, which ends up being tragic for all sides.

CaringBridge.org has helped over 100,000 patients during these difficult times and has impacted millions upon millions of lives. With a mission of "connecting the hearts behind the keyboards," Sona has undoubtedly succeeded in this quest. No amount of money can help at these times, but giving your love, support, and encouragement makes all the difference.

To get involved or get started, just go to www.CaringBridge.org, and please recommend this to any friend who would benefit.

OTHER GREAT USES OF TECHNOLOGY
TO ENABLE PEOPLE TO GIVE:

AmieStreet.com—an amazing, innovative music distribution company (similar to iTunes.com) that has a special program to donate to your choice of charities just for trying their service and downloading a free song. Go to www.AmieStreet.com/ DownloadtoMakeaDifference for more details.

ChangingThePresent.org—Changing the Present has some awesome "charitable gifts" that you buy for your friends instead of the usual bath set or novelty sweater.

GlobalGiving.org—GlobalGiving connects you to over 450 prescreened grassroots charity projects around the world.

GuideStar.org—GuideStar has a huge database of in-depth information about tens of thousands of nonprofits to help you make an informed decision of where to donate.

Idealist.org—Idealist is an interactive site where people and organizations can exchange resources and ideas, locate opportunities, and find supporters.

IDoFoundation.org—Create a wedding gift registry with the I Do Foundation's partner stores, and up to 10 percent of gift purchases will be donated to your favorite charity.

JustGiving.com (www.firstgiving.com is the U.S. site)—Firstgiving is a simple and efficient way to raise money online for charity.

Kiva.com—Kiva is the world's first person-to-person micro-lending website, empowering individuals to lend directly to unique entrepreneurs in the developing world.

NetworkforGood.com—Network for Good has gathered up tens of thousands of your favorite charities all into one system for simplified giving and creative gifts such as their Good Card.

Meetup.com—Meetup.com is an easy way to create and find local groups, including volunteer opportunities in your area.

SmallAct.com (full disclosure: this is the company where I work)— Many ways to give to your favorite charity without having to pay the bill. Start raising money by making this your homepage!

Believing that small acts are the most powerful source of positive social change, Casey Golden's mission is to turn inaction into action by creating simple, easy steps to break the anchors of social complacency. Both professionally and personally, Casey is focused on infusing awareness and understanding into daily life to drive support and participation. He is continually inspired by his family, especially his wife, Beverley, and fifteen-month-old twins, Lilyrose and Tristan. You can read more at his blog, www.SmallActsBigImpact.com.

A Note From the Authors

We hope that these stories of giving inspire you, and remember that all of us can do a little more and consider our giving while living today. Whether in your community or around the world, choose one or more actions that make a difference. Continue to search for meaningful ways to make a difference and connect to causes that matter. Consider what you can do and inspire yourself and others as giving of our time, talents and treasures has never been more critical. We thank our contributors for their stories of inspiration and motivation to live a life of purpose and lift up another person. Live your life on purpose and celebrate and support the core value of this book to "Do Your Giving While You are Living."

www.doyourgiving.com

EDIE FRASER

EDIE FRASER is an internationally acclaimed executive, champion, and advocate for diversity and women and philanthropy. Based in Washington, D.C., she is Managing Partner and Diversity Chair of the largest woman-owned executive search firm, Diversified Search Ray & Berndtson. After service early in her career on the Peace Corps staff and the nation's poverty program traveling to inner cities, migrant camps, and Indian reservations, she joined an international PR firm and directed consumer affairs. As an entrepreneur, Edie built the Public Affairs Group. She founded Diversity Best Practices (DBP). Edie has also served as publisher of major resources on diversity and women. She has published numerous books and publications and given hundreds of speeches. Edie designed the CEO Diversity Leadership program.

A highly sought after board member, Edie serves as a founding member of the Committee of 200; board of SCORE; and the advisory board of Enterprising Women magazine. She is on the leadership circle of three women's political organizations. She is on the leadership board of the National Foundation of Teaching Entrepreneurship in Washington, (NFTE), a past President in Washington of the National Association of Women Business Owners, and the leadership board of EAWC.

Edie Fraser's numerous awards include the following examples: eWomen Network International Femtor Award; Count-Me-In Leader Entrepreneurial Award; Euro-American Women's Council Artemis Award; Enterprising Women Hall of Fame; First Global ATHENA Award; Women of Color Award; LATINAStyle Mentor of Distinction Award. Previously she has received awards from several state governments for supporting women. She also received the Asian American Advocate Award by the National Council for Asian American Business; Minority Business Special Advocate award; Top 50 Americans Minorities award; selected as one of the fifty Americans doing the most for diversity; and The Disabled Advocate by the National Roundtable on Corporate Development for Americans with Disabilities; as well as The Big Brothers Youth Public Service Award.

ROBYN FREEDMAN SPIZMAN

ROBYN FREEDMAN SPIZMAN is a nationally recognized media personality, *New York Times* best selling author, and popular speaker. She has written and co-authored dozens of books including *Will Work From Home: Earn the Cash—Without the Commute* (with Tory Johnson, Berkley Books, 2008) and *Where's Your Wow? 16 Ways To Make Your Competitors Wish They Were You!* (with Rick Frishman, McGraw-Hill, 2008) Considered one of the country's leading gift experts, she is featured often on *The Today Show*. For over twenty-five years, Robyn has reported weekly on the Atlanta NBC affiliate WXIA-TV with her consumer segments, product and book reviews, and began her television career in 1981 as a regular guest on NBC's *Noonday*. Robyn appears on the popular *Cindy & Ray Show* on Star 94 in Atlanta and online daily with "The Giftionary," focusing on gift advice for all occasions at www.star94.com.

A prolific author, Robyn also authored *Make It Memorable: An A-Z Guide to Making Any Event, Gift or Occasion...Dazzling!*, *The Thank You Book*, *When Words Matter Most*, and teamed up with Tory Johnson to co-author *Take This Book To Work: How To Ask For (And Get) More Money, Fulfillment and Advancement* (St. Martins Press, 2006), and *Women For Hire's Get-Ahead Guide to Career Success* (Perigee, 2004). Having written many inspirational books, she co-authored her first work of fiction with Mark Johnston titled *Secret Agent and Secret Agent Strikes Back*, the *Questions To Bring You Closer* series with Stuart Gustafson and the *Author 101*™ series with Rick Frishman.

Robyn's timely gift-giving tips and consumer suggestions have been heard around the country repeatedly on NBC's *The Today Show*, CNN, MSNBC, The Discovery Channel, CNNfn, Talk Back Live, Good Day New York, New York One, and numerous ABC, NBC, CBS, and Fox affiliate stations. Her creative advice and books have been featured extensively in print media including *The New York Times*, *Larry King Online*, *USA Today*, *USA Weekend*, *Women's Day*, *Ladies' Home Journal*, *Parade Magazine*, *Family Circle*, *Redbook*, *Cosmopolitan*, *Delta's Sky Magazine*, *Dr. Laura's Perspective*, *Cosmo Girl*, *Parents Magazine*, *Better Homes and Gardens*, *Entrepreneur*, *Southern Living*, *Parade Magazine*, and many other media outlets.

Nominated for a Book For A Better Life Award, The USA Today Family Channel Award as well as Georgia's Author Of The Year, *Business To Business Magazine* named Robyn one of Atlanta's leading women and a Diva of Atlanta's business world. A popular keynote speaker, she has entertained audiences across the country with passionate and lively presentations on a variety of topics including the topic of giving and making a difference, discovering your wow and other timely ideas of relevance to listeners, employees, organizations and companies around the country. Robyn Spizman serves on the eWomen Network Advisory Council and The Make-A-Wish Foundation of America's National Advisory Council. Robyn is married, has two grown children and lives in Atlanta, Georgia.

For more information, see www.robynspizman.com.

NOTE FROM THE PUBLISHER

*Join Morgan James Publishing
And Help Us Make A Difference!*

Morgan James Publishing's founder, David L. Hancock, recognizes that millions of Americans face a housing crisis. In fact, 5.1 million American families have "worst-case" housing needs, forced to pay more than half their income for housing, endure overcrowded conditions, and/or live in houses with severe physical deficiencies. While the number of families in poverty is growing, the number of affordable rental units is shrinking, and most families who qualify for government housing assistance aren't receiving any aid.

Worldwide, the need is even greater. Some 2 billion people worldwide live in poverty housing. More than 1 billion live in urban slums, and that figure is expected to double by 2030. Many of these people earn less than US $2 per day.

Habitat for Humanity is changing lives. Working in partnership with low-income families to build decent homes they can afford to buy, Habitat helps to break the cycle of poverty and hopelessness. At the end of 2005, more than 1 million people worldwide will live in decent, affordable Habitat for Humanity houses.

In this unique program, Morgan James Publishing is committing to the following and is challenging others to do similarly:

1. Financial support—Morgan James Publishing is donating a percentage of all book sales on a monthly basis from our global (US/UK/CA) efforts under the Habitat for Humanity Peninsula Building Partner Program for the life of each book.

2. Public awareness—Morgan James Publishing is raising awareness by promoting Habitat for Humanity with every book we release, both inside and outside (with authors' consent, of course), and creating press opportunities to promote Habitat for Humanity prominently on our Morgan James Publishing, LLC website(s), literature, radio spots, seminars, etc.

3. Mobilizing volunteers—Morgan James Publishing rolls up our sleeves and does whatever it takes to encourage and mobilize, globally, volunteers with an emphasis on Habitat for Humanity, including getting our own hands dirty!

"We place the Habitat for Humanity logo on the back and inside of our books, with a statement that a percentage of the revenues from the book are donated to the organization. We also give a small library of books to the new homeowners. So at the same time when we are generating funds for them, we are also raising awareness for the organization's life-changing work, helping low-income families build decent homes they can afford to buy."

— DAVID L. HANCOCK

For more information about the Morgan James Publishing Habitat giving program, visit www.MorganJamesPublishing.com.

Printed in the United States
137513LV00002B/15/P

9 781600 374531